JAMES W. JONES

Religion and Psychology in Transition

PSYCHOANALYSIS, FEMINISM, AND THEOLOGY

Yale University Press   New Haven and London

Printed in the United States of America

Library of Congress
Cataloging-in-Publication Data

Jones, James W., 1943–
    Religion and psychology in transition :
psychoanalysis, feminism, and theology/
James W. Jones.
        p.   cm.
    Includes bibliographical references and
index.
    ISBN 0-300-06769-0 (hardcover : alk.
paper)
    1. Psychoanalysis and religion.   2. Fem-
inist psychology.
    I. Title.
BF175.4.R44J655   1996   96-15777
291.1'75—dc20   CIP

A catalogue record for this book is available from
the British Library.

The paper in this book meets the guidelines for
permanence and durability of the Committee on
Production Guidelines for Book Longevity of the
Council on Library Resources.

10 9 8 7 6 5 4 3 2 1

Contents

Acknowledgments / vii

Introduction / ix

I Being Human

1   Freud on Human Nature and Religion / 3

2   The Capacity for Relationships / 24

3   A Relational Psychoanalysis of Religion / 41

4   Toward a Relational Theology / 65

II Knowing

5   Illusion / 97

6   The Dilemmas of Reductionism / 114

7   A Nonreductive Psychoanalysis / 131

Conclusion: Being Human, Knowing God / 151

References / 155

Index / 163

Acknowledgments

At the 1993 annual meeting of the American Psychological Association I received the William J. Bier Award given by the Division of Psychology of Religion. I wish to thank my colleagues for giving me the opportunity in my invited address on that occasion to present publicly my ideas about the dialogue between psychology and religion and to explore the personal context out of which my work has grown.

In October 1994 and January 1995 I was invited to give a series of lectures and seminars at the Rosemead School of Psychology, in La Mirada, California, in which many of the ideas contained here were presented. I wish to thank the faculty, students, and staff of Rosemead who arranged these visits and provided many gracious and stimulating opportunities for discussion. At the other end of the continent and the theological spectrum, during the spring of 1995 I taught a seminar at Union Theological Seminary in New York, and I wish to thank those students for a semester of passionate and fruitful discussion around that seminar table.

Several people read an early draft of the manuscript in its entirety, placing me forever in their debt. Randy Sorenson's comments both encouraged me and forced me to look at familiar material in new ways. Ten years ago Marilyn Saur founded a study group that started me thinking about this topic in new ways. Much of my writing (including this book) would have remained unwritten without Marilyn's feedback and support and that of the group on object relations theory and religion. More years ago than either of us will say, Frank G. Kirkpatrick and I were graduate students together in the religious studies department of Brown University. In the ensuing years our friendship continued but our interests diverged as he delved deeper into the philosophy of religion and I went off to study and practice psychology. But the past few years have found us intellectually reconverging as my studies of British object relations theory brought me to consider the philosophy of John Macmurray, the subject of Frank's lifelong interest. Not only did Frank's careful philosophical reading greatly strengthen the manuscript, but the fruit of his willingness to share his knowledge of Macmurray's philosophy and its relation to the work of W. R. D. Fairbairn and Harry Guntrip and my tremendous debt to it are clear in these chapters. John McDargh served as a reader for this manuscript and, as always, his comments were unfailingly gracious and helpful, not only in his review but in our many conversations over many dinners over many years. Malcolm Diamond, friend, colleague, model of graciousness and courage in the face of life's vicissitudes, contributed to this manuscript through his capacity for truly constructive criticism. Once again Naomi Goldenberg in our continuing discussion of these topics demonstrated that close friendship and ferocious disagreement can co-exist, and my growing impetus to make psychology and theology more sensitive to gender has been reinforced and areas of confusion clarified by these ongoing debates. Charles Grench, a prince among editors, and his colleagues at Yale University Press were, as always, a pleasure to work with. Rutgers University provided me with a faculty academic study leave during which time this book was written.

An earlier version of chapter 5 was published as "Knowledge in Transition: Toward A Winnicottian Epistemology," *Psychoanalytic Review* 79:2, and is used by permission of the *Psychoanalytic Review*, published by the National Psychological Association for Psychoanalysis.

Introduction

This book represents a dialogue between psychoanalysis and theology that has been going on in my mind and with colleagues for more than two decades. As both a clinical psychologist trained in psychoanalytic psychology and a professor of religious studies trained in the philosophy of religion who continues to work in both religious scholarship and clinical practice and who has a background in philosophy of science, this discussion has been central to my professional life. But I am not only an academic. I am a practicing psychotherapist. I have also been an ordained member of the clergy and a student of spiritual disciplines from a variety of religious traditions. So psychotherapeutic and spiritual *practices* have been consciously (and unconsciously) interacting inside me as well. And as a professor of religious studies conversant with many religious traditions, I am inclined, while using predominantly Western theological language, to approach the interaction of religion and psychology from a perspective encompassing world religions rather than just a single tradition. Therefore the dialogue I hope to construct here will take account of both psychoanalytic and religious ideas and also their respective practices (as illustrated by case material) and will take place in a multireligious framework.

Questions put to me regarding my earlier work, *Contemporary Psychoanalysis and Religion,* provided the impetus for this book. Readers raised three major criticisms of that book: first, that Freud was used simply as a starting point and was not discussed in sufficient depth; second, that gender as a category of analysis was overlooked; and third, that the theological implications of my discussion of psychoanalytic theories of religion were not elaborated. I agree with all three and in this book treat those areas left underdeveloped in the earlier work. In the ensuing chapters I analyze Sigmund Freud's model of human nature and theory of narcissism in some detail. I argue that the category of gender is deeply implicated in his theory of religion and that a gender-sensitive psychoanalysis has much to contribute to our understanding of psychoanalytic epistemology and its relation to religion. And throughout this book I keep psychoanalysis and theology in continual dialogue.

Dialogue, as I understand it, is a conversation that respects the integrity of all the participants. From the psychoanalytic side, this book discusses how psychoanalysis might reconsider religion and stay within the psychoanalytic domain. I rule out the explicit incorporation of religious content or practice into psychoanalysis, as found in transpersonal psychology and various religiously oriented psychotherapies. And as important as it is for the sensitive practitioner to take account of a patient's religious orientation, that is not the primary motivation for this book. I wish to show how a reconsideration of religion grows naturally out of contemporary psychoanalytic theorizing. What I seek here is an approach to religion grounded in psychoanalytic *theory*, not just in clinical pragmatism.

From the theological side, dialogue means that religion must be able to interact with psychoanalysis without being reduced to psychology. The problem of reductionism in the relationship of psychology and religion obviously has a long history, going back before Freud at least to Ludwig Feuerbach. And the problem remains very much alive. One question I am invariably asked when I lecture on these topics, regardless of the audience, is whether I am reducing religion to psychology. Chapter 6 is devoted to that problem.

In fashioning my discussion, both tradition and respect now behoove me to start with Freud. Freud had two contrasting but complementary approaches to religious material. In *Totem and Taboo* he gave a genetic analysis of the origin of religion based on the oedipal complex. In *The Future of an Illusion* he gave a functional analysis of the role of religion in the individual's psychic economy based on his theory of narcissism. The first located religion primarily in the superego, the second primarily in the id. Religion had no place in the ego, which was the seat of rationality and the reality principle and so was reserved for natural science.

In this sense Freud's metapsychology is, among other things, an internalized representation of the nineteenth-century conflict between religion (in the form of the childish id and the tradition-bound superego) and science (in the form of the rational ego). Freud's cry "where id is, let ego be" expresses his wish that science replace religion. (For this insight into Freud's metapsychology I am indebted to what I consider the best book on Freud and religion, Judith Van Herik's *Freud on Femininity and Faith* [1982].)

These two Freudian approaches to religion will structure this book. The first chapter lays out Freud's theory of the origin of the superego out of the oedipal complex and the derivation of religion from the vicissitudes of superego formation. Such an exploration will involve us in the various transmutations of Freud's oedipal theory. But this excursion will cast light on the twin themes of this study—religion and gender. Central here are Freud's theory of human nature and the source of religion within it.

Chapter 2 charts the movement from Freud's isolated, instinctual view of human nature to a vision of the self as constituted in and through relationships, bringing with it a refocusing of psychoanalytic theory on the pre-oedipal rather than the oedipal period and a redefinition of individuality and autonomy as relational constructs. This relational model of human nature touches on themes found in a variety of spiritual traditions and opens new perspectives on human experience as expressed in religion.

These shifts in the psychoanalytic model of human nature are intimately involved with the category of gender. Refocusing on pre-oedipal issues involves the displacement of the father by the mother, and moving away from an instinctual model of human nature to an interpersonal one mirrors various concerns of feminist theorizing.

The second part of the book, concerning the epistemological foundations of psychoanalysis, begins with Freud's theory of narcissism. In this context he wrote his most sustained attack on religion: *The Future of an Illusion.* An examination of his argument reveals the ways in which his discussion of narcissism is not only a theory of human development but also an implicit epistemology.

More recently psychoanalysis has turned away from Freud's positivistic and reductionistic method. This turn is clearly part of a more general shift in our understanding of science, paralleled in contemporary philosophy. This epistemological transformation within psychoanalysis has two aspects relevant to the analysis of religion. First, it makes possible a new appreciation of the symbolic. D. W. Winnicott and Hans Loewald, for example, propose independent lines of development for the symbolic order rather than the reduction of all symbolism to the vicissitudes of instinct. This obviously has profound implications not only for the interpretation of religion but for art and literature as well. Second, the problem of reductionism is cast in a new light. Drawing on contemporary philosophy of science, in chapter 6 I revisit the problem of reductionism and propose ways for psychoanalysis to approach religion that are both genuinely psychoanalytic *and* non-reductionistic.

Besides arguing that changes in psychoanalytic models of human nature and epistemology can create a new openness to religious experience, I also suggest that they can provide new resources for theological reflection. One way that religious thought proceeds is by taking some category of human experience (for example, law, history, nature, morality, or consciousness) and making it the key to understanding the experience of the divine. Throughout religious history, the category of relationship has often been central to religious understanding. In the West, for example, such thinkers as Georg W. Hegel, Friedrich Schleiermacher, and Martin Buber (despite their differing definitions of relationality) all use relationality as the basis of their philosophy. Making the experience of relatedness a core creates a convergence between contemporary psychoanalytic theory, some schools of feminist theorizing, and certain themes in religious thought. Chapters 4 and 7 and the conclusion explore this convergence, pointing out the implications of these trends in psychoanalytic theory for religious self-understanding.

I

Being Human

I

Freud on Human Nature and Religion

The Formation of the Superego

Sigmund Freud's narrative of the origin of the superego is, among other things, an answer to the question of how antisocial instincts become civilized. For Freud, human nature begins and ends with pleasure-seeking, biological drives: the building blocks of personality and the source of all human achievement. That starting point forces him to struggle, in the third chapter of *The Ego and the Id,* with how these antisocial drives of Victorian Darwinian theory are domesticated. Drawing on his theory of depression as articulated years earlier in *Mourning and Melancholy,* Freud maps the journey from blind instinct to high culture through the creation of the superego.

Freud proposes that when a significant figure dies or is lost in some other way, the image of this object is taken inside the psyche, where it becomes a part of the ego. This internalization of the lost object keeps alive the attachment, although the connection is now to an internal object rather than an external one ([1923] 1960: 24). Much of the structure of an individual's personality—the things he fears, the goals she desires—results from the internalization of these lost objects, which have a "great share in determining the form taken by the ego and [make] an essential contribution towards building up what is called character" ([1923] 1960: 23).

Depression requires the loss of an object that is both loved and hated, desired and feared. When such an ambivalent object is lost, it is taken into the psyche in order to hold onto it internally even though it is gone in the external world. The positive feelings toward the lost object provide the motivation for its internalization, but the negative affects are now turned inward against the internal object and the ego of which the internalized object has become a part. Depression, which Freud describes as anger turned against the self, is the result.

The most potent of these object losses is the boy's giving up his attachment to his mother as the oedipal drama is resolved. At first, Freud says, the boy is equally attached to both father and mother, but as his erotic feelings for his mother grow, his feelings toward his father become more ambivalent and take on a "hostile coloring and change into a wish to get rid of his father in order to take his place with his mother" ([1923] 1960: 27).

In addition, the boy's ambivalence toward his father is intensified by his fear of castration, the threat the boy assumes his father will visit on him if he attempts to replace the father in relation to the mother. In the "demolition of the Oedipus complex" the boy, fearing castration, gives up his libidinous cathexis to his mother and identifies with his father, internalizing the father figure as the superego or ego-ideal, which is the "heir of the Oedipus complex" ([1923] 1960: 32). In the development of the superego, a lost object "has been replaced by an identification" ([1923] 1960: 23). The internalized father figure compensates for the loss of the mother and strengthens (through the internalized fear of castration) the renunciation of oedipal desires and so defends the ego against their resurgence.

But, as Freud notes, "these identifications are not what we would have expected" ([1923] 1960: 28), for the boy does not internalize an identification with the mother, who is, after all, the lost object who has been given up. Rather, the boy internalizes an identification with the father. To resolve this theoretical contradiction, Freud invokes the idea of bisexuality. In the pre-oedipal period both boys and girls have both masculine and feminine inclinations and so have erotic feelings toward both parents. Consequently the young boy has an erotic cathexis to his father. Freud goes so far as to wonder out loud whether "it may even be that the ambivalence displayed in the relations to parents should be attributed entirely to bisexuality and not, as I have represented it above, developed out of identification in consequence of rivalry" ([1923] 1960: 29). This would mean that the psyche's foundational experiences were relational and driven by attachment rather by ambivalence and loss.

Freud quickly abandons that suggestion and returns to ambivalence toward the father driven by oedipal rivalry as the primary motivation for the internalization of the father and the creation of the superego. But because the pre-oedipal boy (and girl) is bisexual, the dissolution of the Oedipus complex requires the boy to renounce his libidinous cathexis to the father, and so, Freud concludes, in that sense the father too is a lost object whose loss must be compensated for by internalization. Thus the explanation of the origin of the superego remains consistent with the theory of internalization as compensation for object loss, as outlined in *Mourning and Melancholia*. As always, internalized identification replaces a lost libidinous object.

Freud is driven to invoke the category of bisexuality and the tortured discussion of the various combinations and permutations of child-parent identifications (the masculine inclinations of the boy in erotic relation to the mother and in rivalrous relation to the father; the feminine inclination of the boy in erotic relation to the father; the feminine inclinations of the girl in erotic relation to the father and in rivalrous relation to the mother, and so on; see [1923] 1960: 26–29) in order to keep the origin of the superego within the bounds of drive theory. Libidinous cathexis and the rivalries they spawn must alone explain the origin of the superego and, with it, the origin of all religion, morality, and culture. Although he occasionally hints that object relations and identifications with others may exist in their own right, Freud consistently rejects this theoretical direction and returns again and again to deriving social relations and cultural institutions from the more primary drives (Mitchell 1988: chaps. 2–3).

A striking implication of Freud's theory of bisexuality is that the Oedipus complex in girls is resolved "in a precisely analogous way" to that of boys ([1923] 1960: 27). This suggestion, implying a fundamental psychic equality of the sexes, was soon abandoned (in *Some Psychical Consequences of the Anatomical Distinction between the Sexes,* 1925) and replaced by a theory in which the girl is seen as never renouncing her primary attachment (to her mother) or experiencing the fear of castration. Without full renunciation, internalization cannot be complete. Thus the superego, and with it the capacity to create culture, are much weaker in women than in men (see Van Herik 1982 for a discussion of Freud's models of gender identity and their implications).

Freud has trouble maintaining the standard version of the Oedipus complex, in which identification and libidinous object choice are separate, even opposite. Pre-oedipal identification (with the mother) is the same for both genders. The boy must supplant the identification with the mother by a new identification with the father, while the girl remains identified with the primary maternal object both before and after the oedipal or Electra period. For the boy, identification is both the problem (when it is the pre-oedipal identification with the mother) and the solution (when it is the post-oedipal identification with the father). For Freud, pre-oedipal identifications are problematic, and post-oedipal identifications are healthy. Freud downplays the pre-oedipal period and consistently maintains the centrality of the post-oedipal. This dismissal of pre-oedipal dynamics plays a major role in his discussion of religion and morality and motivates his rejection of Romain Rolland's argument for a pre-oedipal origin for religion. For Freud, oedipal processes must remain central.

The boy's post-oedipal identification with the father is profoundly ambivalent. On one hand, the boy is told that he must be like his father, that is, masculine. On the other hand, on pain of castration, he must not be like his father, that is, desirous of the mother. The boy's identification with the father points him toward masculine heterosexuality and lays the basis for normalized, heterosexual object choice. But the same identification potentially intensifies the boy's heterosexual rivalry with the father for the mother. So the father is both the ideal example of masculinity and the feared object of rivalry.

In his discussion of the origin of the superego out of the oedipal struggle, Freud is really describing two intertwined but separate processes: identification with the father and repression of the incestuous wish for the mother. For Freud, identification and repression combine in the dissolution of the Oedipus complex. This dissolution is the source of both social and sexual normalization (through the identification with the father) and of neurosis (through the repression of desire). The formation of the superego represses the oedipal desires and consolidates masculine or feminine identities. The oedipal process is both the repressed and the repressor. Children are originally bisexual. The Oedipus complex is not the result of heterosexual desire but the cause of it. Children become heterosexual as the result of their resolutions of the Oedipus and Electra complexes. As the means of social and sexual normalization, the Oedipus (and secondarily the Electra) complex is the source of heterosexuality, interpersonal bonds, social authority, and religion.

Given the centrality of the oedipal period for later development, the superego (which is the carrier of the oedipal resolutions) assumes a crucial role in mental life. The significance and power of the superego flow from the inescapable dominance of the oedipal drama in the individual's development, which "has introduced the most momentous objects into the ego" ([1923] 1960: 48, altered slightly). The child may internalize many objects, but only the superego, the internalization of the father, has the power to overwhelm the ego and so contribute to neurosis. Although the mother forms the child's first relationship, for Freud the father is the most significant figure in the child's early object world, for an "individual's first and most important identification [is] his identification with the father" ([1923] 1960: 26). The power of the superego in the individual's inner world mirrors the power of the father in the child's early life, for "the super-ego retains the character of the father" ([1923] 1960: 30).

This is especially true when the child is young and the father appears particularly overwhelming. "The super-ego owes its special position [to its being] the first identification and one which took place while the ego was still feeble" ([1923] 1960: 48). The dominance of the father in the family is mirrored by the dominance of the superego in the inner world. Patriarchal family structure has become internalized as psychic structure. The superego "preserves throughout life the character given it by its derivation from the father-complex. . . . As the child was once under a compulsion to obey its parents, so the ego submits to the categorical imperative of its super-ego" ([1923] 1960: 49). The internalization of paternal authority then, in turn, becomes the psychological foundation for pa-

triarchal culture and religion, and patriarchal culture and religion provide ideological rationalizations for paternal authority.

The child is under the dominion of the father. The internalization of
that dominion as the superego becomes the psychological basis for obedience to the laws of culture. The stricter the father and the more authoritarian the culture, the more rigid will be the superego, experienced
as the voice of conscience and guilt. "While the more powerful the Oedipus complex was and the more rapidly it succumbed to repression (under the influence of authority, religious teaching, schooling and reading),
the stricter will be the dominion of the super-ego over the ego later on—
in the form of conscience or perhaps an unconscious sense of guilt"
([1923] 1960: 30). This inevitable guilt is the psychological foundation on
which patriarchal religion and culture are erected.

Freud, of course, attributes the entire process to biological necessity.
Given the boy's inborn erotic attractions and fears of castration, the oedipal dynamic and with it patriarchal culture follow with a natural inevitability like the planets obeying Newton's laws of motion. For Freud
the structures of patriarchal culture express the fixed laws of nature, but
his argument can be read in reverse. What Freud sees as the inevitabili-
ties of nature are really expressions of the structures of patriarchal culture. What Freud uncovers in his discovery of the Oedipus and Electra
complexes is not the physics of the psyche but the internalization of the
structures of patriarchal society as it impinges differentially on boys and
girls (such a reading underlies several of the essays in Chodorow 1989).
The relative passivity that Freud observed in many of his women patients, for example, may not be the inevitable consequence of an Electra
complex whereby women remain identified with their mother in submission to their father and so lay the basis for their own submission to
their husbands. Rather, such passivity may result from the internalization of cultural norms. The observed Electra complex is as apt to be the
effect of patriarchal culture as patriarchy is to be the natural result of biological law.

All the energy within the psyche comes from the id. The force with
which the superego presses down on the id must ultimately derive from
the id itself. In the course of the Oedipus complex, the erotic and ag-

gressive energies of the id, formerly directed at the parents, are directed back at the internalized parental image, which is now a part of the ego. Through the formation of the superego, the ego takes the energy of the id and directs it back against itself ([1923] 1960: 33).

Feelings formerly directed at the father are now directed at the ego. The rage at the father is now experienced as the attack of the superego on the ego, which is felt as guilt. "Aggressiveness is introjected . . . sent back to where it came—that is, it is directed toward his own ego" ([1930] 1962: 70). The superego sets itself over the rest of the ego and turns the "same harsh aggressiveness that the ego would have liked to satisfy upon other, extraneous individuals" on itself. This self-generated aggression against the ego "is called by us the sense of guilt" ([1930] 1962: 70).

To this aggression against the rivalrous father is added the fear of the father's power to castrate. This fear on the boy's part potentiates the power of his conscience. Freud repeatedly reminds his readers that the "superior being, which turned into the ego-ideal, once threatened castration" ([1923] 1960: 60). The terror of castration becomes the "nucleus round which the subsequent fear of conscience has gathered; this dread persists in the fear of conscience" ([1923] 1960: 60, slightly altered).

The fear of castration is a major motivator of the oedipal drama. It explains a large part of the boy's ambivalence toward his father and provides a powerful incentive for the boy to renounce his mother and so begin the process of internalization that leads to the formation of the superego. And this fear of the father becomes transformed into the ego's fear of the superego, which causes the ego to pay attention to the superego's demands. But because the "fear of conscience is a development of the fear of castration" ([1923] 1960: 61), morality and civilization, which are built on the superego, are possible only for men, who fear castration, not for women, who have nothing to fear and therefore no reason to develop a powerful conscience. So Freud insists that the "male sex seems to have taken the lead in all these moral acquisitions" ([1923] 1960: 33–34; for more on this subject see Van Herik 1982).

The process by which the self-centered, antisocial, instinct-driven infant is civilized is also the process by which the infant becomes gendered. The paradigmatic male, like the subsidiary female, begins life identified with the mother. Eventually the father interposes himself between the boy and his mother. The father's prohibition of incest with the mother, backed by the threat of castration, sets up the oedipal triangle. The resolution of the oedipal conflict transforms the male from an id-driven infant into a socialized man able to accept the prohibitions of society. The father's intrusion in the symbiotic mother-son bond begins the boy's journey toward autonomy. Out of fear of castration the boy moves away from symbiosis and into autonomy. The masculine experience of autonomy, then, is tinctured by feelings of loss that have to be defended against in a variety of ways. This is the point at which the feminist psychoanalytic critique of masculinity begins.

Feminist psychoanalysis stands Freud's argument on its head. Seen from its perspective, male, not female, development is problematic. The girl grows up in relation to the mother, thus remaining connected to her primary object. The boy, in contrast, must mobilize himself (usually through aggression) in order to break the identification with the mother. Femininity is thus characterized by empathic connection and caring, whereas masculinity is defined by a defensive need for distance and a denial of connection. Aggression against women becomes the core of masculine self-definition.

Nancy Chodorow's summary can stand as a convenient statement of this position:

> As a result of being parented primarily by a woman, men and women develop differently constructed selves and different experiences of their gender and gender identity. Through their early relationship with their mother, women develop a sense of self continuous with others. . . . The basic feminine sense of self is connected to the world. . . . Men develop by contrast a self based more on denial of relation and connection and on a more fixed and firmly split and repressed inner self-object world: the basic masculine sense of self is separate. The object-relations view argues that as a result of being parented primarily by a women, masculinity develops a more reactive, defensive quality than femininity in women. (1989: 184)

Throughout this book I shall explore how this reversal is founded on a different view of human nature and generates a psychoanalytic reassessment of science and, potentially, of religion.

Having derived the superego from the vicissitudes of the id, Freud is in a position to address questions of religion and morality and, in doing so, to respond to the question of the origin of the spiritual dimension of human life. Freud does not deny that there is a spiritual and moral element in human life, but he denies it any autonomous existence. Conscience, society, and the spiritual life derive from biological instincts and the defenses built against them:

> The ego ideal answers to everything that is expected of the higher nature of man. As a substitute for a longing for the father, it contains the germ from which all religions have evolved. The self-judgement which declares that the ego falls short of its ideal produces the religious sense of humility to which the believer appeals in his longing. . . . The tension between the demands of conscience and the actual performances of the ego is experienced as a sense of guilt. Social feelings rest on identifications with other people, on the basis of having the same ego ideal. Religion, morality, and a social sense—the chief elements in the higher side of man— were originally one and the same thing. They were acquired phylogenetically out of the father-complex: religion and moral restraint through the process of mastering the Oedipus complex itself; social feeling through the necessity for overcoming the rivalry that then remained between the members of the younger generation. ([1923] 1960: 33–34)

Social bonds, moral sensitivities, and spiritual desires are all reaction formations against the antisocial impulses of the id.

Totemic Religion and the Origin of Patriarchy

Ten years earlier Freud had drawn on the oedipal theory to discuss the origin of religion and culture. *Totem and Taboo* ([1913] 1950) casts the oedipal drama backward in time so that the origin of the individual conscience becomes the model for the origin of culture. "In Darwin's primal horde," Freud begins the story of culture and religion, "there is a violent and jealous father who keeps all the females for himself and drives away his sons as they grow up." Once the oedipal situation was set up, the result was inescapable. Eventually the sons murdered the father who possessed all the women ([1913] 1950: 141–142).

Once again, instinct-driven ambivalence is the key—this time to understanding the genesis of culture. The history of culture parallels individual development. After the sons acted out their jealousy and hatred, the other side of their ambivalence emerged: love replaced hate. At first the sons hated their father, who stood in the way of their boundless desire for power and sex. But they loved and admired him too. After murdering him, their affection for him, which they had had to deny in order to kill him, reappeared as guilt and remorse. This is how guilt, on which all religion depends, originated ([1913] 1950: 143). "We cannot get away from the assumption that man's sense of guilt springs from the Oedipus complex and was acquired at the killing of the father by the brothers banded together" ([1931] 1962: 78–79).

The murderous sons of the primal father, the harbingers of all civilization, had to find a way to make peace with their returning repressed guilt. A substitute for the father had to be found. Freud, in his analysis of phobias, already had a model ready: "In every case, where the children concerned were boys, their fear related at bottom to their father and had merely been displaced onto the animal" ([1913] 1950: 128). Like little Hans, the guilty sons projected their feelings onto an animal, and totemism, and with it religion, was born.

> The claim of totemism to be regarded as a first attempt at religion is based on the first of . . . two taboos—that upon taking the life of the totem animal. The animal struck the sons as a natural and obvious substitute for their father. . . . They could attempt, in their relation to this surrogate father, to allay their burning sense of guilt, to bring about a kind of reconciliation with their father. . . . Totemic religion arose from the filial sense of guilt, in an attempt to allay that feeling and to appease the father by deferred

obedience to him. All later religions are seen to be attempts at solving the same problem. ([1913] 1950: 144–145)

A primary tool in psychoanalytic understanding is the search for parallels. The parallels between rituals and obsessive acts, for example, demonstrate to Freud that the same dynamics are at work. Likewise, the parallels between totemic practices and the Oedipus complex are too striking for Freud to ignore. "The two principal ordinances of totemism, the two taboo prohibitions which constitute its core—not to kill the totem and not to have sexual relations with a women of the same totem—coincide in their content with the two crimes of Oedipus, who killed his father and married his mother, as well as the two primal wishes of children, the insufficient repression or re-awakening of which forms the nucleus of perhaps every psychoneurosis. . . . the totemic system . . . was a product of conditions involved in the Oedipus complex" ([1913] 1950: 132).

Totemism is the beginning of religion, patriarchal theism its end. Freud remains convinced that the root of every religion is a "longing for the father" ([1913] 1950: 148). Therefore the first religious object, the totem, can only be a "surrogate father." As time goes on and the primal murder fades into unconsciousness, an object can emerge into consciousness that carries a more complete resemblance to the lost father by embodying the "unlimited power of the primal father against whom they had once fought as well as their readiness to submit to him" ([1913] 1950: 148). This all people call God. For "while the totem may be the first form of the father-surrogate, the god will be a later one, in which the father has regained his human shape" ([1913] 1950: 148).

So, in the last analysis, the so-called higher aspects of human nature are permutations of incest and murder. A "memorable and criminal deed was the beginning of many things—of social organization, of moral restrictions, and of religion" ([1913] 1950: 142). The desire to kill the father lives on as the core of culture: "Religion, morals, society and art converge in the Oedipus complex. . . . the problems of social psychology, too, prove soluble on the basis of one single concrete point—man's relation to his father" ([1913] 1950: 157). Superego masochism is the foundation of morality, religion, and civilization.

The oedipal legacy of patriarchal religion becomes the lens through which all religious history is to be seen. "The god of each of them is formed in the likeness of the father, his personal relation to God depends on his relation to his father. . . . at bottom God is nothing other than an exalted father." ([1913] 1950: 147). Freud, convinced that the murder of the father and its continual replay in fantasy and culture is the hinge on which history turns, can easily read religious development forward or backward from that point.

> There can be no doubt that in the Christian myth the original sin was one against God the Father. If, however, Christ redeemed mankind from the burden of original sin by the sacrifice of his own life, we are driven to conclude that the sin was murder. The law of talion, which is so deeply rooted in human feelings, lays down that a murder can only be expiated by the sacrifice of another life: self-sacrifice points back to blood-guilt. And if this sacrifice of a life brought about atonement with God the Father, the crime to be expiated can only have been the murder of the father. (1913, 1950: 154)

The original theory of the process of internalization in *Mourning and Melancholia* implies that the boy should internalize an image of his mother, because she is the lost object. But in the third chapter of *The Ego and the Id,* Freud complicates the earlier theory (for example, by invoking the category of bisexuality) in order to argue that in dissolving the Oedipus complex the males of the species, the creators of culture, simultaneously renounce their attachment to their mother and internalize an image of their father. For it is the internalized image of the father, as ego-ideal, that is foundation of culture and religion. In the resolution of the male Oedipus complex the connection to the mother is displaced by an identification with the father.

The same displacement of the feminine influence by the masculine takes place in psychoanalytic theorizing, as the pre-oedipal, mother-dominated period is downplayed in favor of the developmental centrality of the oedipal, father-dominated stage. And, keeping to the parallel between individual and cultural development, Freud confesses he can find no place "for the great mother goddesses, who may perhaps in general have preceded the father gods" ([1913] 1950: 149). This oversight surely parallels the fact that he can find no place in his theory for the pre-oedipal, maternal period in human development except its displacement by a normative patriarchy. With the coming of the oedipal period individually and prehistorically, the normative ethos of patriarchy returned. "With the introduction of father deities a fatherless society gradually changed into one organized on a patriarchal basis. The family was a restoration of the former primal horde and it gave back to fathers a large portion of their former rights" ([1913] 1950: 149).

In a letter to Freud responding to *The Future of an Illusion*, Freud's friend Romain Rolland, a student of Hindu religion and biographer of Ramakrishna and Vivekenanda, proposed a pre-oedipal origin to religion in a "feeling of something limitless, unbounded—as it were, oceanic . . . a purely subjective fact, not an article of faith" (Freud [1930] 1962: 11). Freud admits he can find no evidence of this feeling in himself, but he does not deny its existence. Rather, he denies that Rolland has "correctly interpreted it" ([1930] 1962: 12). Rather than a "sensation of eternity," such an oceanic feeling is, for Freud, a residue of pre-oedipal experience before the ego had learned to distinguish itself from the surrounding world. In some people this "primary ego-feeling has persisted to a greater or less degree, it would exist in them side by side with the narrower and more sharply demarcated ego-feeling of maturity, like a kind of counterpart to it. In that case, the ideational contents appropriate to it would be precisely those of limitlessness and of a bond with the universe—the same ideas with which my friend elucidated the oceanic feeling" ([1930] 1962: 15).

Freud, having firmly committed himself to the centrality of the father, the father God, the oedipal struggle, and the masculine gender, must deny Rolland's claim that religion arises from pre-oedipal, maternal dynamics.

> We are perfectly willing to acknowledge that the oceanic feeling exists in many people, and we are inclined to trace it back to an early phase of ego-feeling. The further question then arises, what claim this feeling has to be regarded as the source of religious needs.

To me this claim does not seem compelling. . . . The derivation of religious needs from the infant's helplessness and the longing for the father aroused by it seems to me incontrovertible. . . . I cannot think of any need in childhood as strong as the need for a father's protection. Thus the part played by the oceanic feeling, which might seek something like the restoration of limitless narcissism, is ousted from a place in the foreground. The origin of the religious attitude can be traced back in clear outlines as far as the feeling of infantile helplessness. ([1930] 1962: 19)

The only definition of religion Freud will consider is a patriarchal religion of law and guilt built around the father God.

In the name of this patriarchal religion of the common man, Freud attacks those philosophers and theologians who translate this simple faith into more rational terms.

In my *Future of an Illusion* I was concerned much less with the deepest sources of the religious feeling than with what the common man understands by his religion—with the system of doctrines and promises which on one hand explains to him the riddles of this world with enviable completeness and on the other, assures him that a careful Providence will watch over his life and will compensate him, in a future existence, for any frustrations he suffers here. The common man cannot imagine this Providence otherwise than in the figure of an enormously exalted father. Only such a being can understand the needs of the children of men and be softened by their prayers and placated by the signs of their remorse. The whole thing is so patently infantile, so foreign to reality, that to anyone with a friendly attitude to humanity it is painful to think that the great majority of mortals will never be able to rise above this view of life. It is still more humiliating to discover how large a number of people living today, who cannot but see that this religion is not tenable, nevertheless try to defend it piece by piece in a series of pitiful rearguard actions . . . who think they can rescue the God of religion by replacing him by an impersonal, shadowy and abstract principle. . . . [I] address them with the warning,

Thou shalt not take the name of the Lord thy God in vain! . . . Let us return to the common man and to his religion—the only religion which ought to bear that name. ([1930] 1962: 21)

The atheistic Freud shares with the religious conservatives of his day an antagonism toward the work of more liberal theologians within Judaism and Christianity. His attack on the infantility of religion demands that the most infantile aspects of religion be preserved so they can serve as objects of his polemic. Any attempt to translate religious doctrines into modern terms brings forth from Freud a denunciation worthy of the Prophets: "Thou shalt not take the name of the Lord thy God in vain!"

Freud's analysis of religion depends on a specific image of God. The patriarchal God of law and conscience is the only religion Freud will consider. If he were to give up that paternal representation of God as normative, his argument would lose much of its force. Freud reproduces the exclusive, patriarchal monotheism of Western religion in his theory of the exclusively oedipal and paternal origins of culture, religion, and morality. Freud must insist that religion is essentially patriarchal, for that is the only religion that fits within the frame of the oedipal drama and that can easily be derived from the instinct theory. "Without prejudice to any other sources or meanings of the concept of God, upon which psychoanalysis can throw no light—the paternal element in that concept must be a most important one" ([1913] 1950: 147).

In tying morality tightly to the Oedipus complex so that "religion, morals, society converge in the Oedipus complex" ([1913] 1950: 157) Freud is insisting that morality consists mainly of rules and prohibitions. (The question whether a rationally based morality founded in the ego, distinct from an authoritarian morality based in the superego, can also be found in Freud's writings is discussed in much depth in Wallwork 1991: pt. 4.) Freud's tendency to limit morality to a set of prohibitions, like his restriction of religion to patriarchal theism, follows naturally from the centrality of the oedipal period in his theory. Again, the importance of the pre-oedipal, maternal period has been forgotten. Just as forms of religion may be rooted in pre-oedipal, maternal dynamics, so likewise with morality. Along with a post-oedipal, paternal morality of law and authority, there may well be a pre-oedipal, maternal morality of connection and relationship. An appreciation of the integrity and centrality of pre-oedipal dynamics might point to an ethic of relatedness in which the maintenance of connections between people is more central than the imposition of rules. Such an ethic has been expounded by Jean Baker Miller and Carol Gilligan and taken up by many feminist writers, especially feminist theologians and ethicists. Such a relational, feminist approach to moral reasoning parallels the relational view of human nature found in contemporary psychoanalysis and described throughout this book.

Freud's analysis points to the deep psychodynamic connections between patriarchal cultures, paternalistic deities, and guilt-engendering religions. Such connections, common in the history of religion, are not coincidental but can be explained by the Oedipus complex understood not as biological necessity but as cultural expression. Exploring oedipal dynamics reveals the ways males in a patriarchal culture identify with the father and internalize the motifs of dominance and submission, detached and impersonal experiences of power, and the need for distance. The sacred, when encountered in the context of these masculine identifications, is experienced in terms of dominance and submission and transcendental power and control. And when morality is worked out in the same context, the result again is an ethics of moral principles and law backed up by sacred power and dominance. The result is patriarchal religion of divine law and power in which submission to the law of the father is the primary moral imperative and guilt the main religious emotion. Such a psychodynamic conclusion means that a feminist rethinking of Western religion will involve more than just substituting *she* for *he* in reference to God in theological and liturgical texts. A feminist reformation means transforming traditional models of divine authority and power *and* rethinking the nature of ethics.

Civilization and Its Discontents

In *Civilization and Its Discontents* ([1930] 1962) Freud returns to the latent parallels between religion and culture and their common origin in the oedipal period and the superego. Here the problem is not the origin of civilization and religion but their contribution to neurosis, for a "person becomes neurotic because he cannot tolerate the amount of frustration which society imposes on him in the service of its cultural ideals" ([1930] 1962: 34).

About the impositions of civilization Freud was profoundly ambivalent. On one hand, "sublimation . . . makes it possible for higher psychical activities, scientific, artistic, or ideological, to play such an important part in civilized life" ([1930] 1962: 44). On the other hand, civilization depends on our capacity to suppress our inherent drives. Civilization necessarily opposes our basic nature. Society is dominated by frustration, and "civilization is largely responsible for our misery" ([1930] 1962: 33). Rooted in the superego, civilization is an act of aggression against the ego; culture is inherently a depressive phenomena. Guilt is the sign of the presence of the superego, so guilt forms the core of civilization. Guilt is the "most important problem in the development of civilization . . . the price we pay for our advance in civilization" ([1930] 1962: 81).

Premodern, medieval society was bound together by social control imposed from outside; submission to a higher power defined the moral life. Modern society, in contrast, is characterized by autonomy, in which acting freely *and* responsibly is the highest moral state. Combining freedom and responsibility becomes possible through the internalization of society's prohibitions. The historical movement from premodern to modern culture, which Kant calls the movement from heteronomy to autonomy, is described psychologically by Freud's account of the superego, in which internalized controls replace external authority.

Max Weber describes sociologically the same process, in which modern society, with its emphasis on individualism, depends on the internalization of social controls. Weber's "inner world asceticism" refers to the way modern autonomous men and women internalize the demands of society. When such internalized social control works smoothly, modern people do not even realize that their conscience is the creation of culture through the introjection of society's requirements. Instead, the demands of culture are experienced as natural and inherent. Modern man shows up for work on time, pays his taxes dutifully, and is faithful to his wife, not because a policeman watches his every action but because an inner policemen, called the conscience, is always watching him. Modernization did not lead to anarchy, as the medieval critics feared, because external control was replaced by internal control. The tyranny of king and church was replaced by the tyranny of the conscience (Freud's superego) in the Protestant Reformation.

In the *Genealogy of Morals,* Friedrich Nietzsche (1954) traces the same sequence as Freud. Our earliest ancestors lived in a primitive state of instinctual release. Civilization demands the control of those natural drives. The question of the origin of civilization becomes defined for both Freud and Nietzsche as the question of the origin of civilization's prohibitions against our natural desires. At first these controls were imposed from outside. Later they were internalized, and the frustrations born of renouncing a life of pleasure were turned against the self. For Nietzsche modern society is, in reality, no freer or less controlling than medieval society. Rather, modern society is defined by a more subtle and internal, but no less restrictive, set of prohibitions.

Here Freud and Nietzsche part company. For Freud this internalized social control and renunciation of desire, however costly, are good because they make possible autonomous action and cultural progress. Freud values the reality principle enshrined in science and empirical reason. Nietzsche, in contrast, values the pleasure principle and seeks ways to throw off the prohibitions against nature. The *übermensch* renounces the prohibitions rather than the drives and lives without them, acting only on the will to power.

Freud's analysis of the development of the superego and its definitive role in civilization places him in the company of those nineteenth-century critics of civilization who saw it as something heteronomously imposed on an asocial human nature. Whereas Nietzsche attacks the civilizing impulse as emasculating and antihuman, Freud defends civilization as necessary to human progress.

Although Freud often portrays civilization as primarily a set of external prohibitions, that is not the whole story. The advances represented by culture do not come from authoritarian social control and instinctual repression alone but also from "sublimation," through which the antisocial energy of the id expresses itself in, for example, the paintings of Michelangelo and the music of Beethoven. The capacity for sublimation and the creative act are as much a part of human nature, for Freud, as raw eros and aggression.

This capacity for sublimation is expressed in the very language Freud uses. Always careful about words (he won the Goethe prize for literature), he uses *Trieb* rather than *Instinkt* when outlining his so-called "instinct" theory. The German word *Trieb* comes from the verb *treiben,* which means "to push," and so the primary human motivations are urges that push us in certain directions. But in contrast to an Instinkt, which refers to the fixed and determined patterns of behavior in the lower animals, a Trieb can take different forms. A *Trieb* is, for Freud, completely rooted in biology but is also more flexible than an Instinkt in terms of its possible expressions (the dynamics of sublimation are described in more depth in Wallwork 1991 and Loewald 1988).

Freud's discussion of sublimation underscores the paradox of his oedipal theory of the origin of civilization. Out of the conflict of fundamentally antisocial impulses (lust for the mother and murderous jealousy of the father) comes a costly but beneficial socialization. The energy channeled, by the dissolution of the Oedipus complex, away from lust for the mother is redirected toward intellectual creativity and invention. The theory of sublimation allows the relationship of drive and culture to be read either upward or downward (so to speak). Art, literature, and even science can be reduced downward to their physiological roots. But the drives can also be read upward in terms of their potential expression in the achievements of culture.

Freud on Human Nature

Freud's tortured discussion of the vicissitudes of the Oedipus complex lays bare his fundamental view of human nature. We are creatures of biological impulses pushing relentlessly toward their satisfaction. These drives pit us against each other in Darwinian competition and against the requirements of culture. We are always in conflict: within us is the

incessant metapsychological warfare of ego, id, and superego; from outside of us comes the frustrating impositions of civilization. All our personality, our individual characters and styles, as well as scientific en-
lightenment and artistic creativity, arise from these instinctual conflicts
as channeled through our love for and rivalry with our parents. As the
boy becomes a man he moves from dependency to autonomy, a move
made possible through the renunciation of his lust for his mother and
the acceptance of and identification with the law of his father. As Freud
clearly saw, such a vision of human existence has implications far beyond
the psychoanalytic treatment of neurotic disorders. This vision contains
implicit definitions of society, morality, religion, science, and all human
knowledge. The difference between Freud's theories and the relational
psychoanalytic theories discussed in this book represents not only a differing definition of human nature but also differing moralities, spiritu-
alities, and epistemologies.

    In the coming chapters I shall discuss some of the criticisms of Freud's
drive theory and some of the ways it has been supplemented or replaced
within psychoanalysis (see also Greenberg and Mitchell 1983; Jones
1991a; Meissner 1984). But the issues raised by Freud's theory are alive
and well in other guises. Although biological theory no longer emphasizes instincts and release of tension as major motivators of behavior, an
exclusively biological model of human nature and motivation continues
in the language of genetics. All activity and culture are now seen as arising only from our genes' relentless drive to reproduce themselves. Persons are simply carriers of self-replicating biochemicals. And, like Freud's
instincts, genes are regarded as fundamentally selfish, asocial, and
amoral. All conscious thoughts, feelings, and decisions are actually in the
service of maximizing unconscious genetic self-interest (Dawkins 1976;
Wright 1994). No less than Freud, such theorists regard biology as the final word on human nature. Both contemporary biology and Freud require us to consider whether we must give priority to biological forces in
our discussion of human nature.

    Freud's definition of religion as infantile authoritarianism and his at-
tack on it are not simply addenda to his general theory. Rather, his critique of religion follows inevitably from his basic drive theory as ex-

pressed in the centrality of the oedipal dynamic. A friendly assessment of religion probably cannot be grafted onto Freud's drive theory. A re-assessment of religion requires a radically different understanding of human nature. Or, put slightly differently, the arrival of a different model naturally opens up the possibility, from within psychoanalysis, of re-thinking the analysis of religion.

2

The Capacity for Relationships

A transformed model of human nature that makes possible a more open attitude toward religion on the part of psychoanalysis can be discerned in the theorizing associated with the British object relations school of psychoanalysis and the American school of self psychology. Their thinking moves away from Freud's instinctual model of human motivation and replaces it with an essentially relational vision of human beings.

W. R. D. Fairbairn

This rethinking of psychoanalysis begins with the work of the Scottish analyst W. R. D. Fairbairn (biographical information on Fairbairn is taken from Sutherland 1989). Fairbairn spent almost his whole life in Edinburgh, essentially isolated from the mainstream of psychoanalytic development. Raised in the strict Calvinist orthodoxy of Scottish Presbyterianism, Fairbairn graduated from Edinburgh University with a degree in philosophy in 1911 and decided to become a minister. He pursued graduate studies in theology at London University and in 1914 returned to Edinburgh University to study for ordination in the Presbyterian church.

The war, however, interrupted his plans. Commissioned in the army, he fought during the campaign in the Middle East. While in the army, Fairbairn abandoned his plans to become a minister and decided instead to study psychiatry. Returning to Edinburgh, he enrolled in medical school, undertook a personal analysis, became a psychiatrist and psychoanalyst, and (except for a brief time in London early in his career) practiced in Edinburgh until his death. Throughout his life he was an active member of the church, although he switched to Anglicanism (the faith of his mother) after his father died.

Fairbairn's career is strikingly parallel to that of the Scottish philosopher John Macmurray (biographical material on Macmurray is taken from Duncan 1990). They were virtual contemporaries (Fairbairn was born in 1889, Macmurray in 1891), and both were born in Scotland and raised in a strict Christian orthodoxy. Both took their first degree in philosophical studies. The clergy was their first career choice (Macmurray volunteered to become a missionary but was rejected on medical grounds). Both served in the army in World War I, an experience that crystallized for each man a change in career. Fairbairn went on to study medicine and psychoanalysis, whereas Macmurray took another degree in philosophy and become a professor, first in England and later in Edinburgh. Both remained interested in religion, Macmurray describing himself as having "engaged in a lifetime of religious reflection" (Duncan 1990: 6).

Most striking of all, both approached the problems of their respective disciplines from a standpoint that can only be characterized as relational. In words that Fairbairn could have just as easily said, Macmurray writes that "persons are constituted by their mutual relation one to another" (quoted in Kirkpatrick 1986: 1). The physical sciences, Macmurray argues, are devoted to what he calls a mathematical pattern of thinking, in which the whole is analyzed only in terms of its component parts. The biological sciences are characterized by what he calls the organic pattern of thought, in which the whole organism is primary and the parts are understood only in terms of their functioning within and contribution to the greater organism. Lost in both of these, Macmurray says, is what he calls the form of the personal. Mathematical thinking loses what is uniquely personal by looking only at the parts and missing the whole. Organic thinking loses the form of the personal by subsuming the individual into the totality of the organism and seeing the worth of the individual only in terms of his or her contribution to the whole. Macmurray aims to explicate the nature of a personal, as opposed to a mathematical or organic, form of understanding (Kirkpatrick 1986: chap. 3).

Macmurray does not understand the person in terms of the isolated individual. The mistake of René Descartes, and with him much of modern thought, was to begin from the isolated, thinking, subjective self. Rather, Macmurray says, philosophy should begin from the self as agent, the self in action. The person of action, not the lonely speculator, is Macmurray's model for the self. Whereas the thinker can think in isolation, the actor is inherently involved with others. Thus the self as agent is really the self in relation. Modern philosophy is too egocentric, Macmurray argues, and loses sight of the other. Modern philosophy "completely ignores the second person. It is full of Ego and Meum but it knows nothing of Tu and Tuum. Yet the terms 'I' and 'You' are strictly correlative and their correlation is the proper truth in the familiar statement that human nature is essentially social. The 'I' in isolation is non-existent. The real unity of rational experience on the subjective side is not 'I' but 'I' and 'You' in mutual relation" (quoted in Duncan 1990: 46). In acting, we invariably encounter others and so learn the fundamental truth of human experience: that we exist only in relation. As Macmurray says, "My own existence as a person is constituted by my knowledge of other persons" (quoted in Duncan 1990: 85).

Summarizing his career in his Gifford lectures, Macmurray (1957, 1961) argues for an essentially relational view of human nature. The capacity for personal relationships makes us human. Our uniqueness as a species lies not in our existence as individual subjects of consciousness. Rather, we exist as persons because of our relationships with each other and the world surrounding us. This mutuality of interaction is the defining characteristic of the personal. Selfhood is unthinkable apart from relationship. And neither mathematical and reductive or biological and systemic methodologies and models can give a complete account of the phenomena of a relationship between two centered selves.

Macmurray's metaphysic of the personal provides a philosophical justification for the relational psychoanalytic theories of Fairbairn and other contemporary analysts. Macmurray argues for the ontological priority of the self in relation and insists that the domain of the personal demands its own unique epistemology and cannot be understood in terms of either mathematical and reductionistic or biological and systemic models alone.

In answer to the question at the end of chapter 1—Does biology have the final word on human nature?—Macmurray would clearly answer no. Freudian (and current genetic) theories depend on a mathematical or reductionistic methodology that, according to Macmurray, cannot give an adequate account of such basic human experiences as relatedness or intentional action. These demand a more relational model of human nature. When I choose to act or realize that I exist as a person only in relation to other persons, clear physical and biological parameters are involved, but these do not exhaust or completely comprehend the experience of action or intimacy. (For a clear elaboration of Macmurray's argument in terms of more contemporary philosophy see Kirkpatrick 1994a: chap. 5.)

Macmurray's philosophy implies that psychoanalysts ought to embrace a relational view of human nature, not only because it best explains clinical material but also because it is the most comprehensive and compelling model of human nature available. Macmurray seeks to move philosophy away from an exclusively mechanistic epistemology and to reorient it toward the personal and the relational. In parallel to Macmurray, Fairbairn's revisions of Freud's classical theory can be seen as attempts to move psychoanalysis away from an exclusive reliance on models drawn from Newtonian and Darwinian science and instead to give psychoanalysis an interpersonal basis.

These parallels raise the obvious question of whether Macmurray and Fairbairn influenced each other in any way. McDargh writes, "One of the key influences on Fairbairn in Edinburgh was the theologian John MacMurray [sic]" (1983: 206). In a personal communication, Frank Kirkpatrick (1994) tells me that he has corresponded about this with a Dr. Robert Daly, who knew both Macmurray and his student Harry Guntrip and who discussed this with each of them. Macmurray said he never met Fairbairn, and Guntrip confirmed that Fairbairn and Macmurray never met. Also, Macmurray taught in London until 1944. That year, when he returned to Edinburgh, was the year in which Fairbairn published "Endopsychic Structure Considered in Terms of Object-Relations," in which his theories were presented in nearly completed form. This was three years after he published "A Revised Psychopathology of the Psychoses and Psychoneuroses," in which he announced his object relational metapsychology. Sutherland (1989: 63) suggests that Fairbairn was already reformulating psychoanalysis as early as 1939. Guntrip might have acquainted Fairbairn with Macmurray's philosophy, but Guntrip did not start his analysis with Fairbairn until 1948. It appears that Fairbairn independently worked out his object relational theories before Macmurray returned to Scotland or Guntrip entered his life.

Fairbairn's and Macmurray's emphases on the relational may derive from their early religious training, which stressed the capacity for a relationship with God and with other persons as the essence of human existence. Throughout his life, Fairbairn continued to be involved with religion and the church. Macmurray maintained a long-standing connection with the Society of Friends. Guntrip, Fairbairn's major student and expositor, was also a member of the clergy and a student of Macmurray's. And D. W. Winnicott, too, was an active member of the church of England. Thus, when students of religion and analysts interested in religious issues "discover" that British object relations theories appear more amenable to their concerns than Freud's classical theory, a hermeneutical circle may be involved. For object relations theory was often articulated and elaborated by men with quite conscious religious interests and influences (Melanie Klein is the obvious exception to this generalization). So it may not be surprising to find connections being discerned between object relations theory and certain religious themes.

According to Freud the infant is a totally self-centered id who gradually becomes involved with others as a derivative of their providing him pleasure. The infant relates to the mother, for example, because the mother meets his oral needs through feeding. Over time the developing human being learns to invest some of his or her energy into relationships with others, but even in adulthood these relationships are structured around pleasure seeking and tension reduction.

Fairbairn will have none of this. In one decisive sentence he revises the foundation of psychoanalysis: "Libidinal aims are of secondary importance in comparison with object-relations. . . . a relationship with an object and not the gratification of an impulse is the ultimate aim of libidinal striving" (1952: 60). The basic human motivation is establishing and maintaining connections with others. This is hardwired into the human organism. Pleasure does not lead to object seeking, but object seeking gives us pleasure. Pleasure is not a goal but the result of a satisfying relationship. Rather than being a primary motivation, pleasure is secondary, a derivative of good object relations. Impulses do not go seeking for objects, but objects elicit an affective response. No free-floating lustful energy is stored within us, waiting for an opportunity to discharge itself. Rather, an interpersonal encounter with a sensual other arouses us and stimulates our libido. (For a critique of Freud's position of undirected physiological energy, in terms of current psychological research, see Greenberg and Mitchell 1983). For Fairbairn human nature is relational from the beginning; life is structured around establishing connections, not relieving tensions.

For Freud the object exists only to enable the drive to reach the desired goal of the relief of tension. The actual object is not crucial. Almost anything can serve as an object of instinctual gratification: another person, another's body, one's own body, even (in fetishism) an inanimate object.

Fairbairn does not deny that infants (and adults) sometimes seek to relieve tension, but his analysis of the phenomenon is radically different from Freud's. Because pleasure seeking is not an end in itself, when it is observed in that way it must be a distortion of human nature and not a sign of the true human condition. The pure search for pleasure becomes for Fairbairn a "secondary and deteriorative . . . principle of behavior" (quoted in Hughes 1994: 251). It is only when the need for connection and nurturance is thwarted that the individual turns to the pleasure principle as an end in itself: "Explicit pleasure seeking, [that is] the relieving of . . . tension . . . for the mere sake of relieving tension . . . does, of course, occur commonly enough; but, since libidinal need is object-need, simple tension-relieving implies some failure of object relations. . . . It is, thus, not a means of achieving libidinal aims, but a means of mitigating the failure of these aims" (quoted in Hughes 1994: 251). What Freud sees as the basic fact of human nature, Fairbairn sees as a sign of psychopathology.

Freud's distinction between id and ego is a distinction between form

and energy: the id is pure, formless potency; the ego is an apparatus totally dependent on the id for its activation. This parallels nineteenth-century physics, which divided the world into matter and energy (Jones
1984). Such a distinction makes no sense to Fairbairn. For him, form and
energy belong together. Personality is not forms plus energies but a dynamic whole whose components are energetic, directed toward actively
establishing relationships. Such a model is more in keeping with modern physics, which sees matter and energy was two sides of the same coin
(Jones 1984).

It is no coincidence that Freud developed his drive theory primarily
on the basis of his work with hysterical patients. Hysteria is the disorder
that most neatly fits Freud's theory. In part this is because the theory was
derived from formative work with patients suffering from hysteria. In
hysterical conversion reactions, conflicts over sexual desires are expressed
as somatic symptoms. Psyche and soma are brought close together.

In his paper "Observations on the Nature of Hysterical States" (1954),
Fairbairn again sees relational dynamics where Freud saw biological instincts. Not sexual desire but emotional deprivation is expressed in the
hysteric's somatization. In Freud's classical theory of erotogenic zones,
instinctual tension is understood as attaching itself to the bodily organs
(mouths, genitals, and so on). Such a conceptualization, Fairbairn argues, is itself the expression of hysterical psychopathology. Freud mistakes the symptom for the disease. The close connection between psyche
and soma in which psychological conflicts become caught up with physiological drives is not a fact of human nature but a description of hysterical symptomatology. The rather didactic tone of Fairbairn's 1954 paper
conceals its radical intent. Fairbairn is psychoanalyzing Freud's drive theory, calling it not a discovery of the universal essence of human nature
but an expression of a particular form of disease. Again, what Freud took
as the fundamental biological facts of human nature, Fairbairn analyzed
as signs of pathology.

An additional cultural dimension could be added to Fairbairn's analysis of the drive theory as an expression of the dynamics of hysterical disorders. Hysterical conversions, apparently quite common in Freud's day,
are rare in ours for reasons that make sense in terms of Freud's theory. If

such conversion reactions are the result of repressed sexual desire, that state fits nicely with the condition of women in Victorian society. In present-day society, sexual denial and repression are hardly at the center of the culture. Thus hysterical symptomatology would naturally have declined. So Freud's drive theory and the observations on which it is based represent an overgeneralization from a single clinical disorder, one that is heavily conditioned by the society in which Freud and his women patients lived.

Having attributed the drive theory to psychopathology rather than attribute psychopathology to the drives, Fairbairn does the same with the Oedipus complex. For Fairbairn the psychologically primary relationship is with the mother, not the father. The basic structures of personality are internalizations of the child's relationship with its mother. The child's first object relationship lays down the basic patterns to which all later relationships are assimilated. The child's later relationship with the father simply follows in the pathways established through earlier interactions with the mother. The child's relationships with both parents are equally driven by the need for connection and nurturance, growing out of the infant's dependent status, rather than by the wish for erotic satisfaction or the fear that follows that wish: "The Oedipus situation . . . is not . . . basic . . . but derivative of a situation which has priority over it not only in the logical, but also in the temporal sense. This prior situation is one which issues directly out of the physical and emotional dependency of the infant upon his mother" (quoted in Hughes 1994: 255). Rather than the fulcrum around which all development shifts, for Fairbairn the oedipal period is simply another variation of the relational patterns growing out of the more primary need for connection to others.

If the mother acts in a seductive or stimulating way, the boy child's longing for connection may become sexualized. The same may happen to the girl as a function of her father's behavior toward her. Again, what Freud takes as normative biology, Fairbairn attributes to a specific type of pathological interpersonal encounter. The Oedipus and Electra complexes are just two of an endless series of variations on the theme of the search for connection and caretaking. Their appearance is the result of that search becoming sexualized as a consequence of a certain type of seductive interpersonal encounters.

Oedipal dynamics express rather than determine the relational patterns in a child's life. The wishes, fears, and behaviors that Freud attributes to deterministic biological drives, Fairbairn sees as representative of more fundamental relational needs and experiences. As Fairbairn remarked to Guntrip during Guntrip's analysis, "Castration is really symbolic of a total personality situation, feeling stopped from being oneself, fear of loss of individuality and personality" (quoted in Hughes 1994: 264).

Psychopathology, then, results not from the intrinsic clash of instinctual wishes and fears but from the infant's dependency on the mother and the vicissitudes of that relationship. Not the rational renunciation of instincts but a "satisfactory object-relationship during the period of infantile dependence" is the key to later mental health (quoted in Hughes 1994: 257). The source of neurosis is not the repression of erotic energy but, rather, a childhood "in which the child felt he was not really loved as a person and that his own love was not accepted" (Hughes 1994: 257). The breakdown of a relational tie, not the demands of instinctual gratification, lead to later problems.

It is interesting to note in passing another parallel between Fairbairn and Macmurray. In discussing the development of the sense of self, Macmurray (1961) focuses exclusively on the mother-child relationship and leaves out the father's role. Fairbairn (and Winnicott) also concentrate on maternal influences.

Fairbairn, then, undermines the twin pillars of Freud's classical theory: the primacy of the drives and the concomitant centrality of the Oedipus complex. Again and again, what Freud attributes to inherent instinct, Fairbairn sees as the consequence of interpersonal experience. The result is a fundamental revision of the psychoanalytic view of human nature. Human relationships are not the product of antisocial impulses gradually modified into socially accepted forms out of a compromise between fear and lust. Rather, human experience is structured around the establishment and maintenance of connections with others. It is no exaggeration to say, as Greenberg and Mitchell (1983: 156) do, that the "change in theoretical principles of motivation that Fairbairn is proposing is not trivial; it provides a different conceptual framework for viewing the entirety of human experience."

The biological is now seen as an expression of the relational. As Fairbairn says in his typical epigrammatic way, "It is not the libidinal attitude which determines the object-relationship, but the object-relationship which determines the libidinal attitude" (1952: 34). For Freud the state of biological tension controls the nature of the interpersonal encounter. The relentless pressure of pent-up sexual drive demands genital contact. For Fairbairn establishing and maintaining a relationship with another person is primary, and genital sexuality is a carrier of that relationship. The nature of the relationship (gratifying, frustrating, aggressive, or caring) determines the nature of the sexual experience instead of the drive for sexual release dictating the nature of the relationship.

Freud thought that somatic parts and energies were experienced directly and invariably. An erect penis and an open, receptive vagina had a single, obvious significance. In that sense anatomy is destiny. This is probably a corollary of the Newtonian understanding of science as involving raw data and a correspondence to reality. Today many suspect that there is no raw data or direct apprehension of reality. All data comes to us—to use a cliché in the philosophy of science—theory laden. Experiences are always experienced in some context that shapes and forms them (Jones 1981). Body parts and processes do not appear directly in experience but, rather, are mediated through meanings that, in turn, arise only in an interpersonal context. A survey of why people ingest food or engage in genital contact would surely produce an enormous variety of answers, and most would be far removed from the simple urge to satisfy biological needs.

For Freud, what is fundamental are body-based, sexual, and aggressive id impulses. For Fairbairn, what is fundamental is an interpersonal network. Fairbairn's view is also reflected in Winnicott's often-quoted epigram "There is no such thing as a baby but only a mother-infant dyad." For Fairbairn and Winnicott, the self does not develop directly from such somatic processes as feeding and cuddling but evolves from infant-caregiver interactions. If these instinct-driven episodes carry sufficient parental attunement, they contribute to positive self formation. Their psychological import comes not from their instinctual energy but from the meaning they acquire in the context of early interpersonal encounters.

Thus physical drives are not primary in the sense that Freud wishes them to be, for their significance derives from the way they are structured by, and become the bearers of, interpersonally derived meaning. (This point is discussed in more depth in Jones and Goldenberg 1992.)

For Fairbairn all the structures of the personality are connected with objects that have been internalized. Internalization is not a mechanical recording of impressions, like the taking of a photograph, although his use of the term *internal image* can convey that misimpression. Internalization is an active, transformative process in which experience becomes a part of, and thereby transforms, the ego. In Fairbairn's theory the ego starts off as a unitary reality seeking relationships with whole external objects. Unlike Freud's view of motivation as arising from internal drives seeking release, for Fairbairn the primary object the infant seeks is a whole person to whom he or she can relate as one whole person to another. The infant's primary need is not to gratify its instincts but to be seen and responded to as an independent individual. Such interpersonal moments are the context in which biological satisfaction is experienced. Unsatisfying relationships with external objects create painful relational experiences that are internalized and, because they are painful, split off. The splitting of the once unitary ego is caused by the creation of all these internal objects within the ego, each remaining connected to some painful external object experience. Fairbairn's description of these various internal objects becomes increasingly complex and scholastic.

The child's relationship with the mother, for example, initially has both gratifying and ungratifying aspects. The ungratifying experience is further divided into two additional components: first, a pure experience of rejection, and second, an experience of rejection followed by a sense of hope, destined to be thwarted and frustrated, that the rejection can be transformed into acceptance. So the initial experience of the mother gives rise to three separate internalized objects: an idealized, gratifying internal object; a painful, rejecting internal object; a stimulating, enticing, but ultimately frustrating internal object. Each remains bound to an aspect of the mother or, more accurately, to an aspect of the child's interactional experience of the mother. Such a complex model of the ego's structure is a consequence of Fairbairn's consistently relational model of the ego: every aspect of the personality must be in relation to some object and must express some relational experience. The ego is unthinkable apart from relationships. This view is clearly parallel to Macmurray's philosophy that selves (or in Fairbairn's case, parts of selves) exist only in relation to others or objects.

The parents' behavior in relation to the child makes them candidates for internalization and repression. What is really internalized is the affective relationship or the emotional tone of the parent-child bond rather than the parent as a static thing or object. Although Fairbairn's language is ambiguous on this important point, the thrust of his argument clearly indicates that what is internalized is an object *relation* (Jones 1991a).

For Freud, personality characteristics derive from the drives and the defenses erected against them. For Fairbairn, personality is shaped by the internalization of relational experiences. For Freud, psychopathology results from inevitable conflict between instinctual aims and adaption to the demands of reality. For Fairbairn, psychopathology results from pain generated by unsatisfactory interpersonal relationships and the fragmentation that comes as the individual seeks to remain connected to unsatisfying and warring internal and external objects. In summary, Freud sees social relations as antithetical to human nature and inevitably in conflict with it. Fairbairn sees social relations as definitive of human nature.

Heinz Kohut

This relational model of human nature is made even more explicit in the writings of Heinz Kohut. For Kohut, we are born in relation, and we live and die there. As Kohut says simply, "A self can never exist outside a matrix of selfobjects" (1984: 61). By selfobjects Kohut means those relationships through which we "maintain the cohesion, vitality, strength, and harmony of the self" (1984: 197). Just as, when referring to "objects," Fairbairn was really referring to relationships, Kohut too, when speaking of selfobjects, is really speaking of a particular kind of relationship—the kind that is necessary for a strong sense of self.

According to Kohut there are three fundamental relational needs—he calls them selfobject transferences—necessary to develop a solid sense of self: the idealizing transference, or the need to be connected to a greater, ideal reality; the mirroring transference, or the need for recognition and acceptance; and the twinship transference, or the experience that others are like us. These three experiences are the foundations of, respectively, our ambitions, our goals, and our use of our skills and talents. From our idealization of parental figures comes our capacity for sustained commitment and value-oriented behavior. From having our actions understood and appreciated comes our ambition and ability to set goals. From our experience that others understand us comes our capacity for empathy and friendship and action in the world.

This occurs through a process Kohut calls transmuting internalization. For Freud, the needs of the child are always unrealistic and can never be met but must be renounced. For Kohut, the needs of the child must first be met, then gradually frustrated (by the process of transmuting internalization) so that selfobjects can be internalized as selfstructures. When parents fail to be completely attuned to their children, as they inevitably do, children realize that they must begin to take over some of the parental functions and soothe, comfort, or regulate themselves. These minor parental failures are necessary to encourage children to develop their own inner resources. Thus these selfobject experiences of idealization, twinship, and mirroring are "transmuted" or transformed into the "psychic structures" that make us who we are, that is, our goals, ambitions, values, and capacities for care and commitment (Kohut 1971: 49). Kohut cites examples of mature selfobject relations: an increased capacity to be reassured by a friend's wordlessly putting an arm around one's shoulder, the ability to feel strengthened and uplifted when listening to music, the ability to exhibit joyfully the products of one's creativity in order to obtain the approval of a responsive selfobject audience (1984: 76).

These selfobject needs for ideals, mirroring, and twinship are never outgrown but remain throughout our lives. For Freud, as we mature, we become increasingly independent. Not so for Kohut. In one sentence he rejects the progression latent in all modern psychological theories of development, writing, "A move from dependency (symbiosis) to independence (autonomy) is an impossibility and . . . the developmental moves of normal psychological life must be seen in the changing nature of the relationships between the self and its selfobjects" (1984: 52). Even at our psychologically most developed, we can never move beyond the perimeter of selfobject relations.

For Freud, dependence is to be outgrown. For Kohut, the human needs for dependency, connection, and affirmation are never left behind, just transformed into more mature forms. Object relations are the result not of the biological instincts seeking release but, rather, of the inherent human condition of relatedness and the drive for those empathic resonances that sustain us as human beings. For human life cannot exist in the "absence of that responsive selfobject milieu" (1984: 21).

The distinction between self and selfobjects is important only heuristically. In real life the self and its relationships are one. The priority of the self is simply selfhood, developing and maintaining a cohesive sense of itself. Kohut is clear that this is not solipsism. Kohut is talking about not the isolated self but a self that can exist only in relationship. Selfobject relations are the only means for the preservation and survival of a core sense of selfhood. To repeat Kohut's basic maxim: "A self can never exist outside a matrix of selfobjects." All the activities of the psyche—its actions, relationships, jobs, art and music, philosophies, and religions—are to be understood not as defenses against instincts but as ways of maintaining a cohesive self through mirroring and idealizing connections with necessary selfobjects.

Kohut suggests that dichotomies between autonomy and dependency, individualism and collectivism, that have characterized the modern age are false. There is really no contradiction between individuality and belonging. Actually, belonging to a matrix of selfobjects is necessary for that cohesive sense of self that is the precondition for individuality. In an empathic selfobject matrix belonging and connection accompany individuality and autonomy—one pair cannot exist without the other. We are interconnected, a part of a larger matrix. We exist only as a part of a system of selfobjects. Such a relational model of human nature encompasses the wish to get beyond the dichotomy between individuation and interconnection that has been so salient in modernity.

For Freud, psychopathology arises from wholly intrapsychic factors: the conflict between basic instinctual drives and the demands of social and moral reality represented intrapsychically as the ego and superego. For Fairbairn and Kohut, painful interpersonal relations rather than conflicted intrapsychic structures are at the root of later problems. In a sweeping statement, Kohut asserts that "all forms of psychopathology . . . are due to disturbances of selfobject relationships in childhood" (1984: 53).

For Fairbairn, however, pathology results because these bitter interactions must be taken into the psyche, leading to increasing fragmentation of the ego. For Kohut, precisely the reverse is the case. Fragmentation results not from the internalization of ungratifying object connections but, rather, because bitter object relations cannot be internalized, and therefore the individual fails to develop a strong and cohesive sense of self.

Kohut's theory of selfobjects contains two dimensions: a functional dimension and an experiential dimension (this understanding of Kohut is heavily dependent on Lichtenberg 1991). Selfobjects both perform certain *functions* (such as soothing and mirroring) and evoke certain *experiences* (such as cohesion and vitality). Within self psychology a movement has evolved in the direction of what Stolorow, Bandchaft, and Atwood (1987) call an "intersubjective approach," in which psychoanalysis focuses exclusively on the "unfolding, illumination, and transformation of the patient's subjective world" (Stolorow 1992: 159). This emphasis on subjective experience highlights the experiential aspect of the theory of selfobjects and plays down the functional dimension. In this intersubjective approach, selfobjects are important as the elicitors of subjective experiences rather than as the performers of developmental functions. Thus Lichtenberg (1991) argues for dropping the term *selfobject* and replacing it with the term *selfobject experience*.

Intersubjective theories of the selfobject move the focus of psychoanalysis away from the nature or behavior of the object (for example, is the object empathic or disengaged?), away from the function the object may perform (mirroring, idealizing, regulating), and toward the patient's subjective experience evoked by the object (for example, invigorated or depleted). Kohut's theory of selfobjects, then, points in two different directions. Greenberg and Mitchell (1983), Layton (1990), and others read it as a relational theory, which emphasizes the importance of selves existing only in a relational matrix. Lichtenberg and others, however, see it as primarily a theory of subjectivity, which focuses exclusively on the patient's experiential or subjective world.

Shifting toward an exclusively subjective emphasis clearly differentiates self psychology from the object relational perspective of Fairbairn. Such an intersubjective self psychology is not about relations with external objects or their internalization but, rather, about exploring the contours of the patient's subjective world. In this vein, Ornstein (1991) insists that "self psychology is not an object relations theory." Wolf succinctly makes the same point when he writes, "The selfobject relationship refers to an intrapsychic experience and does not describe the interpersonal relationship between the self and other objects" (quoted in Lichtenberg 1991: 462).

Macmurray made a similar distinction in his discussion of the starting place of his philosophy as opposed to Descartes. Descartes takes as basic the experience of the introspective thinker; Macmurray begins with the self in perpetual communion with other selves. For Macmurray, these two assumptions represent diametrically opposed starting points that lead in opposite directions. Descartes' position ends with an isolated subject alone in the universe, whereas Macmurray's discussion points toward communities of reciprocal concern. Descartes' God is either a postulant of pure reason or the object of an intensely private inward experience. Macmurray's God is found in the midst of communities of mutual care. Likewise, intersubjective methods point the analyst toward a deeper exploration of the patient's subjective experience, while object relational frameworks focus the therapy on patterns of interaction in the transference and across the patient's life.

Stolorow argues that all viable psychoanalytic theories must be "*relational* . . . that is, they should bring into focus the relational, *inter*-subjective contexts in which experiences take form" (1992: 160). A relational theory need not be set against an intersubjective one. All experience takes place in a relational milieu, and that relational milieu obtains its psychological impact by becoming part of the person's subjective world. From such a relational perspective, for both Fairbairn and Kohut the self is one pole of an interaction. A cohesive and vigorous self is one side of a mirroring and affirming dyad. A neurotic self is one pole of a deformed and deforming relationship. A self humiliated and guilty requires a critical and judgmental selfobject bond. A confident and buoyant self reflects approving others, while a self which feels diminished and weak points to a distant and uninvolved selfobject. In all these cases, the self that we are is but one pole of the relationships through which we sustain ourselves.

In object relational and self psychological theories, the dynamics of selfhood are the dynamics of interconnection. And all the self's activities—the goals it pursues or renounces, the intimacies it establishes or flees from, the gods it worships or denies—and the patterns that echo and re-echo through those activities, all reflect the deep structure of the relational self.

3

A Relational Psychoanalysis of Religion

In this chapter I shall discuss how a relational psychoanalyst might approach religious material in therapy, and I shall illustrate some of the interpretative gain that can accrue to the analysis of religious material by seeing such material in terms of relational patterns and dynamics. Chapter 4 will show how such relational psychoanalytic models might contribute to theological reflection.

Psychoanalysis and Religious Experience

The shift from a Freudian to a relational model of human nature has tremendous implications for the investigation of the psychodynamic roots of religion. This psychoanalytic task is clearly and concisely summarized by Ana-Maria Rizzuto: "Properly investigated, under detailed and careful historical reconstruction, God's representational characteristics can be traced to experiences in reality, wish, or fantasy with primary caretakers in the course of development" (1979: 123). The relational model uses much the same definition of the psychoanalytic task as Freud did, although the content has changed dramatically. Interpersonal constructs replace the vicissitudes of instincts as the source "of the individual's private representation of God" (Rizzuto 1979: 3).

Within this interpersonal framework religion is understood as originating not from the need to ward off the return of the repressed or to gratify infantile wishes but from the necessity for every cohesive and energetic self to exist in a matrix of relationships. Rizzuto, for example, draws on Kohut's concepts of a mirroring transference and a selfobject bond to explain the early creation of the God representation out of the experience of the mother (1979: 185–188). Our earliest sense of self, she suggests, grows from seeing our self mirrored in our mother's reactions. If the mirror is cracked or darkened, our sense of self will be distorted. For Rizzuto, this early experience of mirroring that forms the basis of a cohesive sense of self lies at the core of our God representation. All other images that are joined to it in the elaboration of our private God representation are colored by that core mirroring experience (or lack of it) with the mother.

Internal representations are not primarily cognitive but, rather, involve sensory experience, affect, somatic sensation, and memory. An internal representation of the child's mother, for example, may be an amalgamation of sensations of being held and rocked, the sound of her voice and the feelings it generated, and the need to idealize her.

These early internalizations are consolidated into ever more complex sets of representations. For Rizzuto, the representation of God is the apex of the process of consolidating object representations into a coherent inner object world. The internal representation of God is a pastiche, put together from the bits and pieces of object representations that the child has at his or her disposal. The private image of God, Rizzuto says, "is created from representational materials whose sources are the representations of primary objects" (1979: 178).

A cohesive sense of self requires a concept of the Absolute to mirror and focus the self's integrative processes. The term *religion* comes from the Latin word *religio,*" which means, among other things, "to bind together." Psychodynamically religion binds experiences together, consolidating the bits and pieces of a person's inner representational world. Thus Rizzuto writes that the "sense of self is in fact in dialectical interaction with a God representation that has become essential to the maintenance of the sense of being oneself" (1979: 5). Rizzuto studied religious development as it occurs in a Western monotheistic milieu in which the symbol of a personal God is the primary carrier of the experience of the sacred. But even in non-monotheistic cultures, religion may well serve the same psychodynamic function of "binding together" the self. The integrative process Rizzuto describes may be generalizable to cultures using other symbol systems to mediate to their devotees the experience of the sacred source of value, meaning, and purpose.

An example, although not a developmental one, from a non-Western culture also illustrates Rizzuto's point. In certain schools of Tibetan Buddhism the devotees visualize their guru in various forms. The ultimate goal of this exercise is to experience the self dissolving into the presence of the teacher in keeping with the Buddhist teaching about the transitoriness of the self. But before that, visualizing an intimate bond with a master serves to strengthen the devotees' sense of self. (Aronson [1985] and Finn [1992] have written about the object relational aspects of Tibetan Buddhism.) Kakar (1991) describes the same process of self-structuralization through a relationship to a master in Hinduism. Although more explicit in Tibetan practices, in which the guru-disciple unit is visualized as merging with the Buddha and then vanishing into emptiness, the same metaphysic of guru as mediator of the Absolute is also found in Hinduism.

The psychological dynamic seems similar whether it is the Western devotion to a personal God, the Hindu and Buddhist concentration on the master-student relationship, the Sufi's ecstatic embrace of the Transcendent, or the Hare Krishnas' bond with their Lord. In all these religions a relationship is established with a personal figure who mediates a deeper relationship with the Absolute. There is no reason why Rizzuto's analysis of the structuring and centering effects of religious practice and experience, and their developmental transformations, would not apply to all these traditions.

One significant and controversial implication of Rizzuto's work is that everyone in the West, of necessity, forms some internal God representation in order to end the infinite regress of questions about the origin of the world and to consolidate the representational fragments born of his or her early life in the world. The representation is there whether or not the person, as Rizzuto says, "uses it for belief" (1979: 200). Often when students have discoursed at great length to me about how they do not believe in God, I ask them to tell me about the God they do not believe in. And they always answer. They have a very clear idea of who or what God is, even though they don't believe in him or her. And I must observe in passing that their images of God are often of a God that I wouldn't believe in either. However philosophically compelling it may be, for Rizzuto total atheism is a psychodynamic impossibility. Everyone has some image of God, even if they reject it as an object of faith.

Kohut, too, suggests that God may function as one pole of a selfobject bond and that the capacity to "create substitute selfobjects via visual imagery when external reality is devoid of tangible selfobjects must be counted among newly acquired assets" in a successful analysis (1984: 76). This, Kohut acknowledges, leads to a "nonapologetically positive assessment of the role and significance of art and religion . . . which differs from the assessment of classical analysis" (1984: 76).

Some might use Rizzuto's claim that everyone has an internalized image of God based on their object relational development and Kohut's suggestion that God may serve as an appropriate selfobject to construct a psychologically based natural theology. Proponents of such a position might argue that the inevitability of a God representation lays the basis for the inevitability of religious belief. Moshe Halevi Spero (1992) and others who follow what McDargh (1993) calls a "God relational" approach to the psychology of religion make precisely this move. Others, like Benjamin Beit-Hallahmi (1992), are suspicious of object relations theory precisely because they are afraid it lends itself too easily to such theological apologetics. I reject both these concerns. The presence of an internalized God representation in all of us is an empirical matter that cannot be used to argue for or against the reality of the divine.

Starting from the premise that a self never exists outside a selfobject milieu, in *Contemporary Psychoanalysis and Religion* (1991a) I suggest that an experiential image of sacred reality grounds our sense of who we are: the child who feels secure grounds that security in a caring God; the child who feels guilty and terrible grounds that sense of self by reference to a wrathful God; the child who feels estranged envisions a distant deity or dreams of a compensatory, warm and tender selfobject God.

Such a view, I argue, focuses the psychoanalysis of religion on the *affective bond with the sacred* and how that object relation serves as the transferential ground of the self. Such an analysis seeks to uncover the ways in which that relationship resonates to those internalized relationships that constitute the sense of self. Like all relationships, that relationship with what is experienced as sacred is constellated out of the internalized relationships that make up the self. Our relationship to the transcendental reality, or lack of it, enacts and reenacts the relational patterns present throughout our life. The deity may carry an internalized critical parent imago, so that coming into the presence of God re-creates that relationship of fear and judgment. God may function to sustain self cohesion as the perfectly mirroring selfobject. A sense of being one of the favored offspring of the supreme being may mobilize a broken grandiose self. A detached selfobject matrix can be re-created through investing the self in intellectualizing about an abstract world spirit or universal system of energy. A relationship to a chronically unavailable primary caretaker can continue through a perpetually unresolved search for the meaning of life. A warm symbiotic bond can be re-created, or the lack of it compensated for, through the intimacies of a baptism in the Holy Spirit or a merger with the Great Mother or the vast ocean of being.

This relational perspective on the dynamics of religion might help us understand what relationships within the inner object world are made conscious by the language of the sacred as void and abyss and the image of the self forever vanishing in the ocean of being. What organizing themes are disclosed by seeing the Virgin Mary floating on a cloud, or hearing the "sound of one hand clapping, or knowing that the "ways of Tao are effortless"? What introjected relationships are reenacted by being a "sinner in the hands of an angry God," by "walking alone in the garden with Jesus," by "resting in the arms of the Great Mother," by "being grasped by the ground of being," by realizing that "God does not play dice," by resigning oneself to fate, or by "experiencing the state of no-mind"? What inner relational patterns resonate in the koans of Zen Buddhism, the syntheses of Thomas Aquinas and Karl Barth, the tragedies of Homer, and the speculations of the Upanishads? Various inner relational patterns may feed our devotional exercises, meditational disciplines, and philosophical theologies.

A shift to relational models leads psychoanalysis to focus less on the sexual and aggressive motifs in religious symbols and behaviors and more on how religious forms embody various relational themes. In addition, relational psychoanalysis has been moving toward a greater focus on experience, especially on affect (see, for example, Lichtenberg 1989; Stolorow 1992). Stolorow, for one, has argued that among the recent changes in psychoanalytic theory, "most important, in my view, has been the shift from drive to affect" (1992: 162). In keeping with this movement, I have argued that a contemporary relational psychoanalysis should focus on an individual's "affective bond with the sacred," that is, the therapist should attend to both patients' affect and their relational patterns as revealed in their religious material (Jones 1991a).

The following two cases illustrate how, by focusing on affect and on how religious material carries the salient relational themes of a patient's life, a relational paradigm generates new approaches to religious material. These case studies are based on actual people. Except for gender, all identifying characteristics have been changed, rendering the individuals unrecognizable.

A God Looking Over My Shoulder

Phil was a thirty-nine-year-old executive in a publishing company when he began therapy because of severe anxiety and stress symptoms. He appeared in an expensive suit with a monogrammed shirt and silk tie and proceeded to describe himself as a "child of the sixties": laid back, committed to self-expression, and always looking for a party. A year before he had been promoted to director of one of the company's magazines in a highly competitive field after working for the company in various capacities for fifteen years. For the prior five years he had been chief editor of another, more specialized magazine in a less competitive area. There his responsibilities were exclusively editorial; his new job involved making final decisions regarding marketing, advertising, and content. In addition, at the same time he was promoted, the company laid off a significant number of staff members, so that everyone who remained had to do the work formerly done by two or three people. Phil had no way of managing the stress that came with the responsibilities of this new job.

We began with a problem-focused approach to stress management involving relaxation training, ventilation of affect, cognitive restructuring of his expectations about work, and the prescription of physical exercise. He picked up the relaxation training and exercise immediately, which buffered him against the effects of stress. And the provision of a place in therapy where could freely express his anger and frustration about his upper management relieved him immensely.

Whereas I have seen many business executives quit therapy after this symptomatic relief, Phil found himself moving into other areas. He began to wonder why he put so much pressure on himself, adding to the stress of the job. He also became aware that over the past five years, since about the time he had been promoted to editor of the previous magazine, he had been growing increasingly depressed. He had become more distant from his wife and more irritable with her and their two children. That realization led us to consider why, if he was really a hippie, he got into business in the first place and to examine the rivalries within his family of origin.

Phil was the third son of a first-generation Roman Catholic couple. His father was an avid sports fan, and his two older brothers were athletic stars from little league through high school football. Phil also had a younger sister. The four siblings were all about a year and a half apart. Phil developed asthma as a child and as a result was skinny and rather sickly. All his father's attention went to the older brothers, and his mother doted on her only daughter. Phil's mother would take him to the doctor monthly, but that was the only regular time she spent with him alone. On those visits she said little to him and talked mainly to the physician. The older brothers felt protective of Phil and included him as much as possible. Around the dinner table and at extended family gatherings Phil held his own in conversation. But at a deeper level he felt like an outsider.

The father ruled the house with an iron hand. He often repeated the maxim "A man's house is his castle." Phil's father ruled his castle like a feudal lord. He would stir up rivalries among the siblings, pitting them against each other with a constant stream of comparative comments and criticisms. When the four children were all in, or near, adolescence, these dinner-table conversations easily escalated into shouting matches. Phil's younger sister tried valiantly to contribute, but their mother remained silent or busied herself with serving or clearing the table.

Phil's father started his career by working in a gasoline station, and by the time Phil was born, his father owned two body shops, so the family was comfortable but not wealthy. They lived in a working-class, ethnic section of Brooklyn. Upward mobility and financial success constituted the father's religion. Although not educated himself, he saw education as the vehicle of economic advancement and insisted that all his children attend parochial school (for the schooling, not the religion) and college. The older brothers all went to prestigious colleges on athletic scholarship. At the time I met Phil, his oldest brother had gone into trading on Wall Street and was a multimillionaire, and his other brother had gone from playing professional football to coaching for a midwestern team. His younger sister had attended law school and become a prosecutor in New York City.

Although Phil appeared weak when he was a child, other kids did not pick on him because of his brothers. And he could be outgoing and entertaining in conversation, so he always had friends in the neighborhood and at school. But, driven inward by his isolation in the family, Phil took to spending his after-school hours reading in the local library while his brothers were at practices. No one seemed to notice or ask where he went between school and supper. When he reached puberty, Phil's asthma abated. He exercised under his brothers' direction and gained weight, but his father still referred to him as the "runt of the litter." And his interest in books remained. Because he was not an athlete, he could not get a college scholarship. But his grades were good enough for him to attend the best branch of the state university system. He majored in English and writing and turned out to be an excellent poet. By the time he graduated, several of his poems were published in magazines. After college, in rebellion against his father's materialistic worldview, he tried to earn his living as a poet, supplementing his income by working in a restaurant.

He lived in a studio apartment in Greenwich Village. In the same building was a woman named Anne. They dated and, after a year, spoke of marriage. She had a professional background and was a special education teacher. She insisted that Phil get a "real" job as a condition of marriage. This, along with the impending responsibilities of husbandhood, reactivated in him his family's expectation of material success. Although he wanted to teach high school English, he got a job in the publishing business and gradually worked his way up to the management position that brought him into therapy. His brothers had looked askance at him during his days as a poet, and his father had virtually disowned him. Though not as wealthy as his oldest brother or as prominent as his other brother and his sister, now he was obviously a success in business and could meet them as an equal.

Therapy explored how he had internalized and repressed both his father's image as the upwardly mobile son of immigrants and his rivalries with his more successful brothers, and how work had reactivated them. As a result he began to be more detached from his work, "not letting it get to me so much," as he put it. His work no longer had to fulfill a need to remain loyal to the family script of financial success, or to prove something to his father, or to gain parity with his older brothers. At this juncture he began to discuss the conflict within himself between wanting to be a loyal son, an equal brother, and a captain of industry, on one hand, and, on the other hand, his rejection of his family's materialistic values in favor of a life style that was more hedonic and also more self-expressive and, as he put it, more spiritual. By *spiritual* he said he meant more meaningful to him personally and to other people. He was afraid that at the end of his life, having succeeded at business, he would find that he had lost himself and led a meaningless life.

That topic took us into a discussion of religion. Nominally Roman Catholic, Phil's father had no use for religion, and that set the tone for the family. Phil certainly imbibed a distinct view of God from his Catholic school experience. The nuns and brothers were strict, not above beating or publicly shaming students. While Phil was in the elementary grades, school and home conspired together to keep him in a punitive and guilt-oriented milieu. This was the context in which Phil first learned of God, whom he quickly associated with judgment and punishment and the feelings of shame and guilt he felt in the presence of his father, brothers, and the priests at school. Phil's sister went to parochial school until college, but the boys all transferred to public school for high school so the older brothers could play sports on the most competitive teams. In high school, Phil says, he forgot about God and religion.

In college and immediately after, he experimented a little with drugs and various meditational practices but did not stick with any of them. At the time he thought of meditation as another way to get "high." His wife, Anne, came from a conservative Protestant family. Partly in rebellion against her upbringing, she too had engaged in minor drug experimentation in college. They were married by a justice of the peace, and formal religion played no part in their marriage at first. After about two years, about the time Phil got his first promotion to an assistant editor's position, Anne began to talk about going back to church. Phil agreed without giving it much thought, and they attended an evangelical non-denominational community church, which she chose. The preaching in the church emphasized sin, guilt, judgment, and total commitment. Anne felt right at home, but Phil was ambivalent. He went to accompany her but internally discounted much of what he heard.

A turning point came when he was asked to join a Bible study for businessmen that met for breakfast once a week. To his own surprise, he agreed. Again, without thinking about it much, he began to absorb the teaching of this church and, after a year, was asked to lead this Bible study. He found himself getting more and more active in the congregation. When their children were born, Phil and Anne became involved in the Sunday school, and Phil served two years on the governing board of the congregation.

About five years before entering therapy, Phil began to lose interest in the church. Citing increased work responsibilities due to his recent promotion, he withdrew from his leadership roles and, eventually, ceased to attend regularly the Sunday service, offering the excuse that he was too tired from work. Anne accepted this, but it added to the underlying tension in their relationship caused in part by his increasing detachment and irritability.

By the time Phil started therapy, he was no longer involved in the church, and even Anne's involvement was reduced to taking the children to Sunday school. It was in this context that we began to explore the role of religion in his life. When I asked him about his view of God, he said, "I don't want to deal with God; I want to be more spiritual, but I don't want to deal with God." He said he wasn't even sure he still believed in God.

When asked what "dealing with God" meant, at first he listed a series of duties—prayer, Bible study, worship—but then suddenly said, "and besides, I don't need someone else looking over my shoulder all the time." When pressed to say what associations he had to God's "looking over his shoulder all the time," he described a cosmic judge and scorekeeper. I asked if that was all there was to God, and he answered by listing in a rather detached way a series of traditional attributes of the Western image of God, focused mainly on God's role as judge; that is, God was a lawgiver, the punisher of sins and the rewarder of righteousness, and so on. I asked about divine forgiveness, love, and caretaking. He replied in a rather flat tone, "Oh yes, that's true too."

Struck by his detached tone, I asked about his experience of God. At first the replies were rather vague and then, after a long pause, he said, "I never experienced any relationship with God; I talked about it but looking back now I realize I never experienced it. It was just words to me. But people responded to the words so I thought I was saying something. I never really prayed, either, outside of church services or opening a meeting or grace before dinner. Formal prayer was all I did."

In terms of an object relational analysis of Phil's internal God representation, the parallels between his image of God and earlier descriptions of his father were striking. With both he lacked any closeness or rapport. He never felt he could become close to his father or that his father had any time for him or was there for him. The only relationship he had with his father was laden with criticism. He felt he had to prove himself to his father by being a financial success and that he had to prove himself to God through his church activities. In terms of Phil's affective relationship, a distant relationship with an unavailable father was recapitulated in a distant relationship with an unavailable God. The only feelings Phil associated with God were shame and guilt for falling short and not doing enough or being good enough—the same feelings he associated with his father. Also, during the time we were discussing his family dynamics, he denied any anger at his father. When asked about anger at God, the whole idea struck him as unthinkable. His internalized paternal images, augmented by his Catholic school experience, provided most of the material for his early internal image of God. This image was reactivated by the preaching of the community church he and Anne joined and so it "felt right" to him. The church's image of God matched the one he brought to their door, as Rizzuto put it.

His mother seemed to play no role in Phil's image of God, but then his mother played little role in his life. Father was dominant in the family, and she was even more peripheral at family gatherings than his siblings. Her daughter received all her emotional investment. The only time she paid any attention to Phil was when he was asthmatic, and so maternal nurturance was associated with weakness and sickness and being cut off from the more valuable masculine world. As she was not there to buffer him from his father's harshness, so there are no nurturant qualities in his God representation to mitigate the divine harshness. And to relate oneself to these maternal qualities was to cut oneself off from the real world of men.

His emotional connection to religion was more through his role in the congregation than through a direct experience of God. At a deep level he felt at home there because the milieu of the congregation paralleled the ethos of his family of origin. The pastor continually evoked this dynamic by referring to the congregation as a family, and it tacitly felt like Phil's experience of family: ruled by a patriarchal figure represented as God and embodied in the pastor, in which women were peripheral and brothers (the male congregants referred to each other as "brother") competed with each other for the father's approval. The pastor's sermons even subtly suggested that material success was a sign of divine favor and should be sought. Phil's internalized images of his father and brothers clearly played a role in his relation to the congregation. Here Phil could reenact his rivalries with his own brothers with the additional benefit of being able to triumph in this family and gain leadership status.

It was no coincidence that Phil became involved in this church when he was in what Daniel Levinson calls a "settling down" phase of life. After a period of rebellion, Phil began to take on responsibilities of job and family. From an ego-psychological standpoint, God the lawgiver and the congregation with its emphasis on commitment and responsibility served to buttress Phil's unconscious resumption of living under the law of his father.

After a little more than a decade of this life Phil became depressed, despite all the outward signs of success: stable marriage with two children, his own home, recent promotion, active religious life. It happened so gradually he was not even aware of it; he attributed his irritability, sleep problems, and loss of interest to the stress of work.

As we explored this period, it became clear that the part of him that had wanted to be a poet or an English teacher, the hippie inside him who valued a less materialistic and more introverted life, had been repressed in the rush to settle down in his mid-twenties. At night when everyone was asleep, he had occasionally gone to down to the family room and started a poem, but not with the consistency of his youth. In addition he was feeling under more and more pressure to succeed as his responsibilities at home, at church, and at work increased. This pressure came from inside but was reinforced by the demands of his family, his boss, and his pastor.

The source of this pressure could be regarded as the superego in Freud's metapsychology or the internalized representation of his demanding father in Fairbairn's. Such internalizations created an "internal saboteur" (Fairbairn) of great power, which was carried by Phil's representation of God. In relation to God, whose demands were portrayed as perfect and unattainable by the pastor, Phil could again feel like the peripheral child and so mobilize all his energy to overcome that feeling and achieve success through hard work on the job and in the church. His family, his boss, and his pastor were willing to reinforce and take advantage of this high-pressure activity without inquiring about its internal cost to Phil. The same detached, demanding experience characteristic of Phil's relationship with his father characterized his experience with God. Both made great demands and provided no aid in meeting them or mercy when Phil fell short.

As his fear of failure, his guilt, and the internal pressure within him intensified, Phil become depressed. His image of God and religious teaching were certainly implicated in the onset of this depression. God was experienced indirectly as another person "looking over his shoulder" and making demands on him. And the idea of God's omnipresence matched the omnipresent expectations he had of his own performance in every area of his life.

In the course of our exploration of his feelings at the onset of his depression, Phil began to get in touch with his anger at his father through a discussion of his anger at God. He had kept his father and God at a distance, both in his external life and his inner world, so that his anger at them would not erupt. The image of the angry God that he heard about every week carried Phil's own internal anger. At first he rejected the idea that anger at God was even possible, but as we explored his feelings during the time of his becoming depressed, the theme of anger emerged. Phil began to speak of feeling angry at God for asking more of Phil than he could do. A week after he spoke about his anger at God, he brought in a dream (which was a rare occurrence) that obviously portrayed anger at his father. The ensuing sessions focused on his feelings toward his father: a longing for a relationship plus a great deal of rage. Because his comments kept spontaneously alternating between his feelings for his father and the same feelings about God, Phil realized that he had (in Rizzuto's words) both found and created a God in his father's image.

Phil returned to the topic of his fear that the life of a businessman, while monetarily rewarding, was not "meaningful" and that at the end of his life he would look back in despair because he had wasted it. Also at this time, as an outgrowth of his relaxation program, he returned to experimenting with meditation. He bought books on the subject and tried to get up early to meditate. It was hard for him to sustain this. But on the weekends he discovered the deepest and most contemplative times came from sitting in his backyard and looking into the woods that bordered his house. Meditation outdoors in a natural setting seemed to have a more profound effect on him than meditating in the family room at five-thirty in the morning.

During this time his religious quest took a surprising turn. He returned to the Catholic church. The precipitant was a televised mass he happened to see when he was alone on a Sunday morning. It was oriented around devotion to the Virgin Mary, and he found it strangely moving. The next week he noticed for the first time that a Catholic church was situated around the block from his office. He had passed it for years but it had never registered. The parish had a noon mass every Wednesday, which he began attending on his lunch hour. The simple service, with no sermon, did not evoke any images of a demanding or judgmental deity. But what he found most compelling, he told me as we explored his experiences there, were the statues of the Virgin that filled the sanctuary. Images of the mother and child and Marian devotions centered on maternal nurturance and forgiveness were psychologically irresistible to him. Without much therapeutic prodding, Phil could easily see their compensatory selfobject functioning. Images of the wrathful Father God faded and were replaced by feminine images of Mary. He said he could spontaneously pray to Mary, in contrast to the dutiful formality of his prayers to God the Father. Gradually he experienced her as a "presence" (his word) in the church, again in contrast to his lack of positive, felt connection to God. He did not attend elaborate Sunday masses with sermons but stayed with the simple weekday services.

At this point the focus of treatment shifted to his role as a father and his relationship to his own children. He still felt ambivalent about being in business, but he understood more clearly what was at stake for him in this conflict between loyalty to the expectations of his family and his own valuing of literature and the creative life. He began experimenting with finding ways to keep them in balance, taking some time to write and using some of the money he made to buy books of poetry and attend occasional writers' workshops. Given the demands on his time by work and family, these were not fully satisfactory. He also reported being more detached at work. He still found the deadlines stressful, and the week the magazine was due often brought a recurrence of insomnia, but he certainly felt less harried and was taking better care of himself physically and psychologically.

For our purposes the main focus of this case is on the vicissitudes of Phil's religious journey, which can be divided into four parts. First came childhood and adolescence, when he first learned of God in a familial and ecclesiastical context characterized by shame and guilt, which he abandoned outwardly as soon as the opportunity arose in high school.

Second was Phil's period of settling down, in which he joined the community church and found an image of God compatible with the one from his childhood. This image of God and the ethos of the congregation strengthened his resolve to take on the responsibilities of adulthood.

But did so in a way that carried heavy internal and external overtones of condemnation and repressed other aspects of himself. Here the affective tone of his religious life was characterized by shame, guilt, and self-deprecation. In these ways his religion contributed to his depression. While supporting his move in the direction of greater maturity and responsibility, in this phase his religion recapitulated his family experiences and was primarily an expression of his deeper dynamics.

The third period was that of agnosticism when, in an attempt to free himself from his depression, he withdrew from as many carriers of that internal demand system as possible: he left the church, ceased to believe in God, and was less involved with his family.

Fourth, his discovery of a more nurturing and forgiving piety centered on the feminine figure of the Virgin Mary. To some extent these nurturing qualities were incorporated from his marital relationship. While Anne, by his report, could be perfectionistic and obsessively efficient, she could also be warm and playful with him and their children, and she was consistent in her concern for his well-being. Although this new object relation contributed immensely to his growth, his new religious milieu did not simply recapitulate his psychodynamics but also actively contributed to a positive psychological reorientation by bringing simpler and more nurturant images and experiences into his life. In this instance his religious practice was a positive, causal factor in his psychological development.

Besides calling attention to some of the positive and negative functions of religion, this case also illustrates an approach to religious material that concentrates on affective themes as well as internalized objects.

The God Who Isn't There

Maxine, known as Max to her friends, appeared in my office complaining of chronic depression. A tall woman with dark features and short hair, dressed in slacks and a sweatshirt, Max was a pediatrician in a public clinic in the South Bronx. For two years she had been engaged in a running battle with her former husband, also a physician, for custody of their son, Joshua. She said that this chronic legal struggle plus the demands of a long commute and of treating some of the most impoverished patients in the country, left her feeling drained. She was finding it harder and harder to get up in the morning. Although she could talk energetically about the importance of her work and spoke with genuine care for her patients, she struck me as rather unemotional and seemed to describe her life as though it had happened to someone else. She was suspicious of therapy as self-indulgent and a diversion from political activity, and she considered taking medication a sign of weakness.

She began describing the conflicts surrounding the custody of her son. He lived with her under a joint custody arrangement, but the boy's father was constantly going to court to try to win full custody. Most of the actual fighting—the discussions with lawyers, the arranging for witnesses, and paying the bills—was done by Maxine's mother. This led us into a discussion of her family. As a young man in his early twenties, her father had been an instructor at a technical school in Germany. As both a Jew and a Marxist, he feared the growing strength of the Nazi party and fled Germany for England in 1933 at the age of twenty-two, just as Hitler came to power. He never spoke about his family, but everyone believed that they had been killed in the holocaust. Ashamed of his German ancestry, in England he took the name Joel Martin to wipe out any trace of his German roots (Martin was the name of the English family who took him in). He came to the United states in 1938. Although he had only technical school training, he was an inventive scientist and eventually got a job with the fledgling IBM corporation, where he worked all his life. By the time he retired, he had several patents to his name. He remained a lifelong and dogmatic Marxist.

Joel arrived in this country knowing no one and worked odd jobs. One was in the warehouse of a small wholesale garment distributor. The owner had come to this country from Poland years before but still spoke fluent German. He had a sixteen-year-old daughter, Miriam, who promptly fell in love with Joel, who was in his late twenties at the time. Her father, a traditional Eastern European, disapproved and fired Joel. They carried on a clandestine relationship when she went to college in New York two years later, and when she graduated they threatened to elope. Her parents recanted, and they were married when Miriam was twenty-two and Joel was thirty-five. Maxine was born two years later. A younger brother, Jacob, was born two years after Maxine, but he apparently developed mild schizophrenia in his teens. A brilliant mathematician, as a young man he would occasionally become delusional and wander the streets in a confused and unkempt manner. He eventually committed suicide.

Maxine described her parents' marriage as stormy. Her mother was moody and demanding, her father always at work. Even when he was at home, Joel spent most of his time in his study in the basement, from which he would emerge at dinner time to harangue the family about current events and, especially, the evils of capitalism, even though he was working for IBM. He paid no attention to Maxine but spent at least an hour a day tutoring Jacob in math and science and then quizzed him mercilessly over the dinner table.

Maxine went to college in New York City in the late 1960s and immediately became involved in radical politics, including the takeover of a building. Her college roommate was involved in a robbery and shootout with police and was sent to jail. Shaken by the feeling that her roommate's life had virtually ended at twenty-one, Maxine withdrew from political activity and decided to apply to medical school, where she was easily accepted. In her first course she meet Leon, the brightest student in the class. By the end of the term they were sharing an apartment. After graduation they were married in a civil ceremony attended only by a few friends. Leon did not go on to be an intern but went directly into research; Maxine interned and did a residency in pediatrics and began working at a community clinic in the Bronx. She also joined a radical feminist study group that met every Sunday.

Both Leon and Maxine were absorbed in their work and rarely saw each other. After five years of marriage, when they both were established in their respective careers, Maxine became pregnant with Joshua. Because she was unwilling to give up her work, they took a student into their apartment who watched the baby in exchange for room and board. When Joshua was two years old, Maxine came home unexpectedly one evening and discovered that Leon was having an affair with this student. A huge fight ensued, and Leon and the student moved into an apartment together. Maxine's mother had moved to the suburbs after Maxine's father died (the same year Joshua was born), and, needing her mother's help with Joshua, Maxine moved near her and commuted to the clinic every day. There began a bitter battle for custody of Joshua, which was to go on for years. In the midst of her adjustment to her new life, Maxine came to see me.

After a year of therapy, Maxine took a two-month leave from her community hospital to do volunteer work at a clinic in South America run by a politically active Christian group. Although she knew that the clinic was run by a religious institution, she was not prepared for their level of piety. The clinic sponsored such political activities as community organization, plus literacy classes and free medical care, but it also held weekly Bible studies and Sunday services.

Upon her return she wanted to discuss religion. She was confused by how much she had in common with the religious group in South America despite feeling alien in their world because of their piety. She began by repeating her received Marxist denunciation of religion, but it sounded hollow to her in light of her South American experience with active and politically committed believers. She wanted to be disdainful of their beliefs but couldn't quite bring herself to be so. She also envied the confidence with which they went about their work. Yet she found their devotion incomprehensible.

I asked about her own religious upbringing. At first she denied vehemently ever receiving any. But during the next session she began to talk about her maternal grandfather. A devout Jew, almost always in a black suit and hat, with a long gray beard that looked as though it was never trimmed, he had appeared to her childish eyes as an ancient prophet or a rabbi out of the Talmud. For all his formality, he was a warm and emotional person, probably the warmest person in her family circle. He would tell stories from memory from the Bible or, more often, from the various strands of tradition. Each story was animated with large arm gestures and changing tones of voice for different characters. Maxine recalled listening happily and attentively as he wove a magical atmosphere around them.

Her maternal grandfather died when Maxine was in junior high school. Long before that, her father had forbidden her brother to have anything to do with the old man. "He's poisoning Jacob's good scientific mind with all that superstitious nonsense," Joel would scream when his wife was taking their children to visit her parents. "Make sure you keep my son away from that senile old man." Apparently her father wasn't worried about Maxine's mind, and she would go happily up to the old man's room on the top floor to listen to his stories.

She confessed that she used to replay his stories in her mind and had created a whole fantasy world with a God-figure modeled on her grandfather—a benign old man with a long beard. Into this world she withdrew to escape her mother's outbursts and her father's tirades.

This private but enchanted world was destroyed by her grandfather's death. Not only did his dying remove the stimulus for it, but, at a deeper level, the loss shattered her young faith. At first, she said, she kept trying to re-create his stories in her imagination, but gradually they became fainter in her mind. In addition, when I asked her how she felt about her grandfather's death, she began to show emotion in therapy for the first time. She became very sad and described how, as a girl, she had lost interest in her studies and her grades had dropped. This brought her father's attention in the form of lectures and scoldings. She also remembered becoming withdrawn from her friends for the rest of the school year. Clearly she had become quite depressed, but no one had noticed. Also she soon entered puberty, relatively early, and the excitement of going out to parties with boys quickly provided a new escape from her home.

So the world of her imagined God faded. As she recovered it in therapy, she was at first disdainful and angry and embarrassed that she had ever engaged in such fantasizing. I kept commenting on the intensity of her anger at herself. She repeatedly justified it by reciting sarcastic comments about religion, which turned out to be virtually verbatim repetitions of things her father had said.

Because this anger was the first real emotion I had seen from her, I kept the focus there by commenting that I was struck that she was so angry at herself for something that was a normal part of childhood development. Even children, she replied, should not be prey to such irrationalities. I then commented on how angry she was at religion itself. I told her I could certainly understand skepticism but I was perplexed by her vehemence and hostility. Again she repeated a string of paternal invectives and said she probably learned her views from her father. "That's certainly true," I replied, "but his anger seems to have struck a cord with you." She was silent for a long time and then began describing more of her father's anger at religion, recalling specific neighbors he had ridiculed and things he'd read in the press about religion that infuriated him. I asked if she knew why religion evoked such rage in him. She didn't know but surmised it was because he'd lost his family in the holocaust. I asked for her reaction to his anger, and she became confused. She said it made no sense for him to be angry at a God he didn't believe in, but his anger seemed justified to her at some other level that she couldn't quite describe. After struggling for a few minutes with what sense it might make for her father to be angry at a God whose existence he denied, she suddenly changed tone and began a tirade against religion as the oppressor of people. Again I commented on the intensity of her anger, which was certainly understandable in light of the historical atrocities committed in the name of religion, but I still wondered whether that was its only source. I added a comment about the connection between anger at God and loss in her speculations about her father and wondered if there wasn't a similar connection in her experience. "You mean the death of my grandfather," she said. "Exactly," I replied.

She was silent for a long time, and the anger seemed to leave her. When she spoke next she talked softly about her grief at his death and her subsequent anger and how, after her grandfather's death, she became more sympathetic to her father's atheism. She clearly was angry at God, however irrational that seemed to her, for her grandfather's death and the loss of her imaginary world.

In subsequent sessions she talked about changes in her life after that point. She had always attributed these changes to puberty and to entering high school two years later and had not seen any connection to her grandfather's death. She had became rebellious at home and in school and was sexually active. She enjoyed the way her rebelliousness frustrated her father, who always saw himself as a rebel and nonconformist but could not countenance the same in his daughter. In college she became involved in even more radical politics than her father. And even when she became less overtly active, her attitude remained hard and angry.

I asked her what she most missed after her grandfather's death. She started to say his stories but soon slipped into discussing her times of making up stories for herself in her own head. I commented that it seemed as though all her imaginative play stopped with his death. She agreed curtly. I asked if she missed it and she said no, of course not, it was all childishness.

About this time in the treatment her dispute with her former husband heated up again, and much of the therapy was taken up with supporting her through this and helping her make decisions about her son. She also began to feel the need to pull back a little from her work, to restore some balance in her life and to have more time with Joshua. In the course of the next year, she reduced her overtime work, went into the city to see movies on the weekends when Josh was with his father, and took over from her mother some of the responsibility for the legal maneuvering. The topic of religion faded into the background. It was not until we began our period of termination that it reappeared.

At that time I asked if she had thought any more about religion, God, and the changes brought on by her grandfather's death. She said she had not thought much about God. She could not imagine ever believing in God. When I asked her about the God she didn't believe in, she was quiet. Then she said, "I just can't get the picture of my grandfather out of my mind. He was the one person growing up who was really *there* in my life, and then one day he wasn't there. That's just how I feel about God; maybe he was there in my childhood, like an imaginary actor in my imaginary dramas, but that was childhood. That's where God belongs. He's just not there any more."

"Has anything taken God's place?" I asked.

"No. There's just a big blank space," she said and then sat in silence. As she sat there her face turned sadder and sadder, as if she were going to cry (she had vowed the first day never to cry in therapy, and she kept her promise the whole time). I asked what she was feeling.

"Sadness, just sadness," was the reply.

"Is that what's taken God's place?" I asked. She was quiet for a long time. "Yes," she finally answered in a new soft voice, "exactly. Sadness, that's what I think of when I think of God. Sadness and emptiness, because there's nothing there."

In the following weeks we occasionally spoke of God, but Maxine insisted that she could never believe in God. The very thought brought up such pain and loss that she had to change the subject immediately. She couldn't allow even the topic of God to be present too long, or the sadness would become unbearable. However significant were her intellectual reservations about God, they rested on a deeper connection between the idea of God and the experience of loss and pain. So close was this association that nothing connected with God could be allowed in her life.

During termination she also talked about the meaning of her work. In medical school she'd sworn that pediatrics was the one field she would never consider. She had no interest in children, and, besides, "caring for kids is women's work," she had said derisively. No sexist stereotypes for her. But after her pediatric rotation in an inner-city hospital, she had been drawn against her will, or so it seemed to her, to spend a summer volunteering at a pediatric emergency service, for she had been unable to get the images of those under-cared-for children out of her mind. After that the course of her life's work was fixed.

When asked what was most attractive to her about her work, she described what she did in terms that were more nurturing and maternal than technically medical. Comforting, caring for, and protecting were more salient in her description than treating and curing. She began to realize that over the last couple of years she had begun to act differently in different settings. In public, in the emergency room for example, she was brusque and efficient and critical of anyone else's shortcomings. But alone with a child in her private cubicle, she was playful and tried to make the examination into a game. She would even tell the patients stories, just as she did Joshua. I remarked that there was something of her grandfather's world in her practice. Here his warmth and playfulness came out in her.

Her original motivation for her work was political and ideological: she wanted to help the poor and oppressed. There had been a tone of righteous anger in her description of her work, especially when she contrasted it to her former husband's academic research or her classmates' suburban practices. I remarked once about this righteous tone and asked if she had any associations. She said no. I asked about her father's ideological rage at capitalism and religion. She remarked sarcastically about her father's hypocrisy in working for IBM and then carrying on like a radical. Also, she said, she felt that her father's anger was purely negative, purely destructive. He simply wanted to tear everything down. She felt that her own anger was constructive: she wanted to reform, not demolish. "Just like the prophets in the Hebrew Scriptures," I remarked in passing.

That passing remark stayed with her until the next session. She had remembered her grandfather's quoting the prophet Amos in a thundering voice—"Woe to those who sell the needy for a pair of shoes"—and at his funeral she found out that although his business had prospered beyond his dreams, he gave a sizable amount of money to the synagogue and its associated charities as well as to employees who were in financial trouble. I commented that her righteous anger was more the anger of her grandfather than of her father and that her motivation to go into medicine in order to care for the less fortunate was more an expression of her grandfather's ideals than of her father's politics.

Although her demeanor softened considerably in the course of therapy, she was never able to overcome the feelings of loss and anger associated with the experience of God. It was hard for her, as well, to enter into the worlds of imagination and play for herself, and she only did so as ancillaries to her roles as pediatrician or mother. These emotional dynamics accounted for her continuing atheism more than did her father's ideological influence. Within the envelope of her atheism, much of her grandfather's religion survived: in her outrage at injustice, in her desire to use her training to care for the needy, and in her playfulness with her patients.

The cases of Phil and Maxine illustrate some of the ways a person's religious experiences or lack of them can carry the same relational patterns present in other areas of their lives. The clinician might approach religious material, then, by obtaining a feel for patients' relational patterns within their religious worlds and listening for echoes of the same relational themes in other parts of their lives.

4

Toward a Relational Theology

Beyond the implications of a relational model for the *analysis* of religious themes (as illustrated in chapter 3), a new view of human nature is being proposed within relational psychoanalysis that has extensive ramifications not just for the psychoanalytic study of religion but for religion itself. Freud's view foreclosed the possibility of a religiously meaningful understanding of human nature. The mechanistic account was complete; all aspects of human life, from the hunger pangs of infancy to the paintings of Rembrandt and the theories of Einstein, were permutations on the themes of sex and aggression. In contrast, a relational model reopens the possibility of a spiritually significant view of human experience. A relational model of human nature affects religion in at least two ways. First, by seeing the self as inherently interrelated and by underscoring the importance of subjectivity, relational psychoanalysis creates the possibility of a more open attitude toward, if not a rapprochement with, religion. Second, such a relational understanding of human nature potentially contains new resources for theological reconstruction. In this chapter I explore some of this potential for theological reconstruction found in these relational models.

The Importance of Religious Experience

In different ways the work of Fairbairn, Kohut, Winnicott, and others shifts the focus of understanding from a concern with biological, instinctual behavior to the nature and quality of subjective experience. Fairbairn, Kohut, and Winnicott suggest that it is the quality of the infants' relational experience of the mother (and later the father) that tips the developmental balance toward later maturity or difficulty. Likewise, the goal of analytic treatment shifts from coping with instinctual demands to facilitating more enriching and authentic forms of experience. This shift reaches its furthest development in the intersubjective theories of Robert Stolorow, George Atwood, and others. (This point is discussed in depth in Mitchell 1993: chaps. 1, 3.) As Stephen Mitchell writes about these theorists, "Psychoanalysis has been undergoing not merely a modernization of its delivery system but a fundamental shift in focus. . . . In psychoanalysis as practiced in our world, the patient's sense of meaning and value does matter . . . what has become central is the emergence, development, and enrichment of the patient's sense of subjective meaning" (Mitchell 1993: 31). Relational psychoanalytic theory is not just a new, more interpersonal philosophical anthropology. It goes beyond that to transfer our attention, in varying degrees, from biology to subjective experience and to redefine the human dilemma in those terms.

To the solution for this sort of dilemma religion has potentially much to contribute. As long as the human problem was defined in such biological terms as the direction or suppression of instincts, religion (like the rest of culture) could enter the picture only as an agent of social control and domination. If the human dilemma primarily concerns the capacity for subjective experience and its enrichment, than religion has more positive and constructive things to say.

Long before the advent of depth psychologies, the religious traditions of humanity developed sophisticated cartographies of human consciousness extending from the elaboration of inner states in Tibetan Buddhism to the writings of Von Ruysbroeck and John of the Cross in the West. Such schemata of consciousness were broadly empirical in the same sense that psychoanalytic theorizing is. They were drawn from disciplined and sophisticated reflection on direct human experience in the context of categories refined within a community over many generations. As the richness of experience replaces the management of libido or the strengthening of the ego as the goal of therapy, psychotherapists can be expected to develop an even greater interest in and attention to the explorations of human creativity and consciousness on the part of the various spiritual traditions. Evidence for this development is the increasing interest in those spiritual disciplines that aim at the transformation of consciousness (especially those drawn from various schools of Buddhism) on the part of psychoanalytically informed clinicians (see, for example, the papers by Finn and Rubin in Finn and Gartner 1992; and Epstein 1995).

As psychotherapists focus more on subjective experience, the accepted psychoanalytically oriented definition of religion will, of necessity, change. Seen through the lens of Freud's theory, with its exclusive focus on instinctual control, religion was understood to center on law, morality, and oppression (especially in the area of sex). This definition of religion as moral law fit in nicely with the patriarchal traditions that Freud knew firsthand and with his exclusively oedipal theory of religion's origin.

If the central human problem is the capacity for experience, however, the core of religion will be defined in terms of religion's ability to expand or constrict human subjectivity, and attention will shift from the legal religion of morality to the mystical religions of direct experience. This returns us to the debate between Freud and Rolland over the nature of religion. The history of religions demonstrates a tremendous diversity of forms of religious expression. The Gita, for example, the sacred scripture of devotional Hinduism, describes four equally potent ways to the experience of the divine: (1) Karma Yoga, or the way of moral action; (2) Bhakti Yoga, or the way of devotion to a personal savior; (3) Ynana Yoga, or the way of philosophical reflection; and (4) Raja Yoga, or the way of disciplined meditation. The choice between them is made not on the basis of spiritual truth but on the basis of individual temperament. Some people are inclined toward concrete moral activity, others toward cultivating mystical transformation, others toward penetrating philosophical insight.

Although all major religious traditions clearly embody all four, some traditions accentuate one way to the detriment of the others. Many kinds of Islam, Judaism, Confucianism, and some types of Christianity have at their core the image of active moral obedience to divine law as the essence of true religion. Other forms of Christianity, as well as the Hare Krishna sects of Hinduism, call forth bhakti, or devotion to a personal savior. Other strands within Christianity, Judaism, and Islam, in parallel with many types of Buddhism, promote disciplines leading to mystical experience. Freud's negative allegiance to a legalistic monotheism and Rolland's insistence on mystical oneness as the core of religion can be placed within this spectrum of world religions as two examples of the many forms of religious expression.

Put another way, the debate between the followers of Freud and adherents of various relational theories over the psychoanalysis of religion has a *theological* as well as a psychological dimension. Such a debate represents not only two different models of human nature, and two different approaches to psychodynamic theory and practice, but also two different definitions of the nature of religion. When Fairbairn, Winnicott, and Kohut shift the focus of psychoanalysis from instinctual control to the quality of experience, this shift parallels the difference between a religion oriented toward law and obedience and a religion oriented towards the transformation and expansion of consciousness.

A model of human nature that sees the self as embedded in a network of relationships, which sees positive as well as negative aspects to connection and interdependence, which orients us more toward the importance of subjective experience, which champions the deepening of interpersonal encounters, contains the possibility of a more open approach to, if not rapprochement with, religion. The connections in which we are embedded may include a connection to a larger, sacred reality without doing violence to human selfhood, because selfhood and interconnection are not antithetical but potentially mutually strengthening. Likewise, dependency on a higher power may not contradict individuation, as the need for interdependence stays with us all our lives. The deepening of interpersonal relationships may lead us to the experience of the sacred. And to the extent that religious practices facilitate the enrichment of conscious experience, they can contribute positively to health and growth.

Freud envisioned human nature in terms of the atomistic science of his day. Each individual was a self-contained system of forces and mech-

anisms. This isolated individualism, when combined with Freud's reductionism, left no place for the spiritual dimension of human experience except as a derivative of biological drives. Winnicott, Fairbairn, Kohut and other relational theorists relocate individuality in a relational
matrix, redefining autonomy as a relational term (Jones 1991b). In keeping with this redefinition of human nature as essentially relational, the
religious dimension of human experience can be located precisely in that
fact of relatedness. In different ways the philosophers Buber and Macmurray argue that a relational vision of human nature (like that found
in relational psychoanalysis) points toward a reconsideration of religion
and of God.

Buber's Relational Theology

"In the beginning is the relation," writes Martin Buber in *I and Thou*
(1970: 69). Like Fairbairn, Kohut, and Macmurray (who was influenced
by Buber; see Kirkpatrick 1986: 141), Buber begins from the primacy of
relationships rather than the primacy of individuals. For all these men,
individuality arises out of relational experiences instead of relationships being simply the result of a meeting of basically unconnected
individuals.

Buber is less concerned than Fairbairn and Kohut with the psychodynamics of human relationships and more concerned with the philosophical and spiritual implications of the fact of our relatedness. Relationships, Buber says, can take two forms, which he calls the "I-it" and
the "I-you." The verbal structure of this distinction might lead one to
think that Buber divided the world into two classes—"yous" and "its,"
persons and stones. In fact, Buber is doing exactly the reverse. The difference between the I-you and the I-it is not the object but the "I"—I am
different in an I-you or I-it relationship. In the I-it, I keep myself aloof,
detached, uninvolved. I see the other as a means of achieving my prede-
termined goal. In the I-you, I am involved, caring, committed. I respect
the other's freedom and autonomy.

Because the difference lies not in the object but in the stance I take
toward the object, I can have a "youish" or "itish" relationship with any

object. Buber (1970), for example, writes poignantly of youish relationships with trees and stones and other natural objects as well as with people. This claim of Buber's parallels Kohut's discussion of selfobjects (this point is discussed in more detail in Jones 1991a). For Kohut, anything can be a selfobject if it sustains and supports our self-cohesion. It may be another person, but it may also be a piece of music, a special text, or a natural wonder. When religious traditions, for example, venerate a sacred text or tree or sculpture or draw on the powers of music, these objects are functioning as selfobjects in Kohut's terms. For Kohut something becomes a selfobject not because of the nature of the object but because of our capacity to relate to the object in a certain way—a way that allows the object to function for us in a self-sustaining manner. As Kohut says, nurturing food is not enough; we also need the capacity to metabolize and digest it. Likewise, the presence of such selfobjects as caring people or beautiful works of art are necessary but not sufficient; to be nurtured by them, we must possess enough psychic structure to internalize the experiences of care or beauty and allow them to feed us psychologically.

In Buber's terms, it is the capacity to relate to objects in a youish way that allows them to function as selfobjects for us. But there are important differences between Buber's and Kohut's theories. For Buber, the capacity to relate in a youish way is innate; it is our primary way of approaching all the objects in our world. For Kohut, the capacity for mature selfobject relationships is not given but, rather, develops over time out of the internalization of positive selfobject experiences in our early years.

Kohut the analyst is much more aware than Buber the philosopher of the possibilities of psychopathology and how it might affect the philosophical and religious quest. The exclusive fascination with the world of the I-it, which Buber finds so problematic about modern society, may be the result not simply of cultural choice but also of psychopathology. Buber is more sensitive to how culture can corrupt the capacity for relatedness (by overvaluing the I-it domain); Kohut is more aware of the effect of individual psychopathology in undermining human interaction through a lack of selfstructure.

The dichotomy of culture and character, however, may be overdrawn.

The relentless detachment of modern culture represents both a constellation of social forces and a personal style characterized by a brittle, defensive autonomy or overly compliant personalities or both. The itish ethos of modernity and contemporary personality styles that are predisposed toward detachment are connected by the process of internalization and the construction of the self out of internalized object relations. Through the process of internalization the cultural ethos is transformed into the structures of selfhood. Internalization, in which our experiences are incorporated into our developing sense of self, is the bridge between culture and the psychic life of individuals.

As the cultural ethos of detachment, control, and efficiency insinuates itself into family life, child rearing is increasingly governed by these same constraints. The child's early experience begins to resemble that of Harlow's paradigmatic monkeys. The emotional tenor of family relationships is the primary factor internalized, and the incorporation of an atmosphere of detached efficiency leads the offspring of modernity to develop selfstructures predisposed toward further disengagement. Then, a narrow-minded reliance on technical efficiency alone can easily take root in personalities deformed by being raised in an atmosphere of detachment. The worship of autonomy and efficiency provides ready rationalizations for these itish styles of being in the world. (This dynamic interplay of culture and character is a major theme in my 1995 book *In the Middle of This Road We Call Our Life,* in which it is more amply discussed and illustrated.)

Smith (1985) argues that the major difference between Buber and Kohut is that for Buber a relationship involves the self in relation to an autonomous other, whereas for Kohut a relationship means that the self includes the other within itself through an empathic extension of the self's boundaries. On Smith's reading Buber's is a philosophy of pure relationality in which, in the I-you relationship, the self becomes devoted to another, whereas in Kohut's theory of the self-selfobject relationship, the self "psychologically includes the other as a functional object" (1985: 254). Smith argues that Buber stresses the importance of entering "into moral relationships with the independent other," whereas Kohut advocates becoming a "self which is capable of knowing itself and the world through an extension of its boundaries" (1985: 253). For Buber the self "seeks to be related morally to the independent other"; for Kohut the self "psychologically includes the other within the self" (1985: 254).

Smith does not see these as antagonistic, however. He argues that a comprehensive theory of selfhood requires an account of both elements of human existence: the capacity to be devoted to the welfare of the other (which Smith calls our "moral" potential) and the capacity to incorporate the experience of the other into our sense of self and know the other empathically through an extension of our own experience (which Smith calls our "psychological" potential). This dichotomy, which parallels Freud's distinction between object love and narcissism, may itself be problematic. Layton (1990), for example, suggests that such a dichotomy, central in both Freud's and Kohut's theories, is the result of a patriarchal and capitalist culture that dichotomizes loving and working, relational desires and instrumental actions. Writes Layton, "Oppressive socialization practices of a culture biased toward agency result in the *appearance* of two separate lines of development [narcissism and object love] . . . [this] *appearance* is already a sign of pathology" (1990: 428). Thus a dichotomy between the "pure" relationality of Buber and the expansive selfhood of Kohut, like the dichotomy of object love and narcissism, may be a reflection more of a cultural penchant for dichotomizing than of any developmental necessity.

Buber is not a romantic or a moralist, insisting that all relationships should be of the youish type. I may have only an instrumental relationship with the attendant at the gas station. We meet briefly only as functionaries: he fills the tank of my car and I give him money. There is nothing wrong with that. The problem comes, Buber says, when we become so involved in the I-it world that we lose the capacity ever to relate youishly.

This is spiritually crucial because, for Buber, the only way to God is through our youish relationships. Buber calls God the "eternal you," by which he means God is eternally you. Buber's central theological maxim is that "the eternal You cannot become an It" (1970: 160). This statement is not so much about God as about our relationship to God. God can only be approached youishly. Whereas in even the most intimate human relationships Buber sees a dialectic of itish and youish moments, in relation to the true God only youishness is possible.

Not through abstract speculation or repetitious ritual but only in the midst of I-you meetings can God be encountered. Buber uses the analogy of a poem. Through reading a poem, or several by the same writer, with sensitivity and openness, eventually one glimpses something of the personality of the poet. One cannot spell out rules for determining exactly when that happens. Some people may have a better eye for poetry than others and may pick up the author's style more quickly. One may not be able to specify exactly when and how one first glimpses the character of T. S. Eliot's work or that of Adrienne Rich. Despite this lack of rule-governed specificity (the itish mode), through reading many of an author's writings, one encounters something of his or her self. Likewise, for Buber, through developing a sense for the youish dimension of life, a person also develops a sense for the divine. Only through cultivating youish relations with people and nature will the eternal you be seen.

That the eternal you cannot become an it defines how God can and cannot be approached. To deal with God from a nonrelational, detached, or invulnerable position is to relate not to God at all but only to an idol, a finite thing put in the place of God—a concept, an abstract principle, a transitory feeling. Thus philosophy and theology, no matter how pious, become for Buber the first step toward atheism, for they approach God as an idea or concept rather than as a personal presence who can be encountered only relationally. In the meeting with God, Buber writes, "man receives, and what he receives is not a 'content' but a presence" (1970: 158).

Buber's philosophy, in which God is met only through personal relationships, is one example of how relationality might become central for religion. And Buber does not simply advocate relationality. Rather, he calls on all of us, psychotherapists included, to examine more deeply what our experience of relationship really is. The botanist relates to the tree as an object of scrutiny and control. That is fine for his purposes, but nothing of spiritual significance will come from that relationship. Only when we relate to others youishly can we encounter God in the heart of those youish relationships. Only through relating to the world in a youish way can we see through all our youish encounters to the eternal you who stands behind them.

Buber, then, articulates a view of human nature as essentially relational. "There is no I as such," Buber writes, "but only the I of the basic word I-You and the I of the basic word I-It" (1970: 54). The I exists only in relation to other objects. This view is similar to Macmurray's, in which persons exist as persons only by virtue of relationships, and Fairbairn's, in which the ego and all of its components are always tied by relationship to some object. Buber's theology is relational in two senses. First, God is known only as we allow ourselves to be in a personal relation to him. Second, we come into relationship with God through our youish relationships with objects in our world, for "extended, the lines of relationships intersect in the eternal You" (1970: 123). God encompasses all relationships; all relationships meet in the divine embrace. The term *God* denotes that other who is addressed in every youish relationship (1970: 123), the third partner in every dialogue.

For Buber (and Macmurray), God is known through deepening reciprocal relationships of mutual concern (Kirkpatrick 1986: chap. 5). To the extent that relational psychoanalytic theories support a similar relational view of human nature and that relational psychoanalytic practice has as one of its goals increasing the capacity for attuned and empathic relationships, relational psychoanalysis and relational theologies work hand in hand. Buber and Macmurray both illustrate how a relational anthropology (like that found in contemporary psychoanalysis) can serve as the basis for a relational theology.

Macmurray's Relational Philosophy of Religion

Along with developing a unique philosophy of the personal and applying it to questions of politics, ethics, and epistemology, John Macmurray wrote about religion all his life. Duncan goes so far as to suggest that Macmurray's "constant pre-occupation with the importance and reality of personal relations . . . represents the religious strain which goes back to the unqualified assertion that God must be conceived as personal" (Duncan 1990: 45).

How does Macmurray get from personal relations to God? For Macmurray, thought is not abstract speculation but reflection upon action. Thus he rejects the search for God through metaphysical analysis or introspective mysticism. God is not an object of abstract thought. For Macmurray, speculative questions about whether God exists arise only from the position of the isolated thinker. Religion must begin instead from active participation in experience. What is the immediate active experience from which religion begins? It is the creation of personal relations. As Macmurray says, "Religion must be concerned with the original and basic formal problem of human existence, and this is the relation of persons. Since religion is a reflective activity, this must mean . . . that religion has its ground and origin in the problematic of the relation of persons, and reflects that problem. In this case religion is about the community of persons" (Macmurray 1961: 157). By basing religion on reflection about "fellowship and community," Macmurray says, he is deriving religion from "facts of direct, universal experience" (quoted in Duncan 1990: 136).

Religion begins with the experience of and reflection about human relations, for the "field of religion is the field of personal relations" (quoted in Duncan 1990: 137). Immanuel Kant, with his reduction of religion to ethics, might have said the same thing. Macmurray, however, rejects the Kantian attempt to reduce religion to moral action alone. Religion, for Macmurray, must be about God, and about God understood in personal terms. He writes, "God is therefore necessarily personal. . . . There can be no question of an impersonal God. The phrase is a contradiction in terms" (quoted in Duncan 1990: 33).

Religious reflection, for Macmurray, begins from concrete human relationships but goes beyond them by seeking to understand relationships in general, which requires a generalized set of symbols. Such an analysis "universalizes" the problem of understanding human relationality (1961: 168). A universal understanding of human relationality requires a symbol of that universal relationality—an object who can stand in direct relationship to every person. This can only be a personal God who is a "universal 'Thou' to whom all particular persons stand in relation" (Macmurray 1957: 72).

God must be personal a thou because, according to Macmurray, we cannot understand the personal in impersonal terms. Human community requires a "personal Other who stands in the same mutual relation to every member of the community" (Macmurray 1961: 164). The whole matrix of human relationships can be bound together only by a "universal person to whom the self stands in universal relation" (quoted in Kirkpatrick 1970: 156).

Human community can be created on the basis of a common ideal or goal. But what Macmurray is talking about is not only common human experience but, rather, what he takes to be the single essential common human experience: the experience of being in personal relationship with others. What makes persons persons is not some universal essence in which they all participate or some ideal they all share but, rather, another person to whom they all relate.

For Macmurray, then, by a close analysis of what it means to be human, we discover the fundamental fact of our relationality. By reflecting on that fact, we are led to envision human persons as existing in a network of relationships. By further reflection on the fundamental reality of a network of relationships, we are led to the need for a universal personal other; that is, we are led inevitably from human relationality to human community to God.

Although Macmurray's argument sounds rather abstract, with its focus on the need to symbolize and represent community by a universal symbol, at another level he is pointing to a deep connection between our experience of our self as personal (that is, endowed with consciousness and intentionality) and the reality of God. Macmurray writes, "The question of whether the world is personal is the question of whether God exists. . . . the theological question is improperly represented in the form, Does God exist? It must be expressed in the form, Is what exists personal? . . . More simply, if we distinguish ourselves—that is, all finite personal individuals whatever—from the world, we have to ask whether the world is personal or impersonal" (Macmurray 1957: 214–215).

The claim that the question of God's existence is, in some sense, the same as the question of the reality of the personal makes sense because the experience of ourselves as persons seems intimately connected with the reality of some source to ground that self-experience. Psychologically this deeply felt connection between our human reality and a personal power or source may be expressed in any number of philosophical ways. Macmurray's insistence that personal reality cannot be totally explained or encompassed by the impersonal domain (that is, by natural science) points to the same connection. So does his argument that human rationality, to make sense, requires a personal other to whom all stand in relation. Behind these philosophical discussions lies, I think, a deeper perception—that personhood is not self-explanatory or completely reducible to deterministic physical processes and that it instead points beyond itself to a more universal, encompassing personal reality known as God.

Models of Relationship, Models of God

In his book *Together Bound* (1994), in which he draws on Macmurray's philosophy to propose a relational theology, Frank G. Kirkpatrick describes three models for the relationship of God and the world: monism, dualism, and pluralism. The term *monism* comes from the Greek term for "one," not in the sense of the first number in a series but in the sense of unity or oneness. In Kirkpatrick's reading, monistic philosophies suggest that beneath the diversity of ordinary experience lies a unity in which all differences eventually disappear. As Kirkpatrick says, "Monism is the claim that, essentially, there is only one reality, undivided and undifferentiated" (1994: 21). The central terms in this philosophy are *undifferentiated* and *incomprehensible:* reality is ultimately without distinction or differentiation and is, therefore, beyond our comprehension. In the imagery of the Indian Upanishads (the most uncompromisingly monistic text in the history of religions), ultimate reality is an ocean to which individual souls, like drops of water, return and are swallowed up.

Because the ultimate is beyond all distinctions, it is completely incomprehensible to us, for we understand only by distinguishing one thing from another. If we cannot draw distinctions, make definitions, or use categories, we cannot understand. Although we cannot intellectually comprehend or understand the Absolute, we can still experience it. For the monist, experiencing ultimate reality means going beyond discursive thought to a state of consciousness in which all categories and distinctions disappear. Thus, Kirkpatrick rightly notes, monism is not in the first instance a claim about the existence of a special metaphysical reality, an ultimate unity, or transcendental oneness. Rather, it is primarily a claim about a special *experience,* in which the mind is driven into a state of consciousness in which all categorization vanishes. Whether one moves from the experience of undifferentiation to a claim about the existence of an all-encompassing undifferentiated reality is a matter, I suppose, of temperament and logic.

Such an approach to ultimate reality by means of direct inward experience or states of consciousness has a certain obvious appeal to psychologists—especially, perhaps, to those inclined toward the intersubjective forms of relational psychoanalysis. Psychologists are apt to be more interested in exploring states of consciousness than in following extended metaphysical arguments. Also, making experience, rather than doctrine, central resonates to those trends in contemporary psychoanalysis that make the enrichment of experience a primary goal of therapy. For these reasons, monism, in some form, may have a natural appeal to the psychologically oriented.

The key term in the dualist's position is *transcendence.* Dualists argue that God transcends the world of space and time, standing outside of and beyond the ordinary world. But such a totally distant God has little religious significance. Thus, religiously inclined dualists must affirm that God relates to the world while simultaneously retaining his transcendence of the world (the masculine pronoun is intentional, for transcendent deities tend to be masculine for reasons discussed in Jones and Goldenberg 1992).

Kirkpatrick finds the dualist position ultimately incoherent, as it wants to maintain two contradictory things: that God is completely beyond the ordinary world and that God is related to or active within the ordinary world. Kirkpatrick argues that, historically, dualistic theologies tend to so stress divine transcendence that God's relationship to and interaction with the world become increasingly hard to understand and appear logically problematic. Dualists are often driven by the internal stresses and contradictions in their position to describe God's relation to the world in frankly paradoxical terms. Such terms as *relationship, love,* and *act* are called analogies or symbols when applied to God. Dualists must spend a great deal of energy trying to explain exactly how a totally transcendent God is and is not related to the world and how such relational terms as *love* and *care* apply and do not apply to God. Kirkpatrick does not find this task worth the effort. (A discussion of the concept of divine transcendence from the standpoint of a gender-sensitive psychoanalysis can be found in Jones and Goldenberg 1992.)

The third position, Kirkpatrick's own, he calls pluralism. This position abandons the monist's insistence on divine incomprehensibility and the dualist's insistence on transcendence (except in the modified sense that an agent can be said to be more than his or her actions and so to transcend them). Kirkpatrick rightly sees that divine incomprehensibility and transcendence are different versions of the same claim: that God is completely beyond finite human categorization. Rather, Kirkpatrick argues, God ought to be conceived "as a distinct, individual being with whom [we] are in relation" (1994: 26). Such a God is a "personal Agent . . . in literal relationship with other beings" (1994: 27). Here one can see the influence of Macmurray. For Kirkpatrick, in keeping with Macmurray's thought, all relationships, even the relationship of God and humankind, involve the interaction of personal agents who act and interact with others in a network or community of "persons in relation" (the title of Macmurray's Gifford Lecture).

These three views of God are also three different models of relationship. The monistic relationship is one of fusion and merger, in which autonomy and individuality disappear like drops of water in the sea. The dualistic relationship is one of distance and separation, in which interaction becomes paradoxical and problematic. The pluralistic relationship is one in which relatively autonomous agents interact with, and thereby limit and condition, each other. We might arrange these three models along a typology with the monistic at one end (the most fused), the dualistic at the other (the most distant), and the pluralistic in the middle. The pluralist maintains a degree of autonomy (which is lost in the monistic experience) in balance with interaction and interconnection. In words used earlier to describe relational psychoanalytic theory, in the pluralistic model autonomy is a relational concept (Jones 1991b).

Such theological reflection forces us to think more deeply about what *relational* really means in a discussion of a relational psychoanalysis of religion (or any aspect of human experience). When discussing relationships, do we emphasize fusion, separation, or interaction? The theological model, drawn from Macmurray, that Kirkpatrick champions seeks to balance autonomy and interconnection. The same drive to overcome the dichotomy between individuality and interrelationship can be discerned in contemporary psychoanalysis as well as in feminist thought and in other areas of contemporary culture (Jones 1991b).

For Kirkpatrick and Macmurray, the term *community* carries the balance of autonomy and connection; a true community is neither a fusion in which selfhood is lost nor a collection of loose psychological atoms without real bonds. In true community (be it an intimate pair, a family, an organization, or a society) individuality is respected and interconnection sustained.

Is Kirkpatrick's pluralistic model of semi-autonomous agents living together in community the only way to keep individuality and interconnection in balance? A similar image emerges from models of organic systems. A living organism is a single system made up of semi-autonomous interacting parts. Such an organic image has been central in the development of general systems theory, which, in many instances, grew from work in the biological sciences.

Like Macmurray, Kirkpatrick is suspicious of systems models, because he feels they tend toward a monistic-like absorption of the individual into the whole. On Kirkpatrick's reading, systems theories are always in danger of seeing individuals only as functions or parts of a larger organism (like limbs of a body) rather than as centers of choice and action in mutual relationship. He asks critically, "Does an organism subsume persons in relation: is the relationship itself an organism greater than the individuals in relation? If so, what protects the uniqueness and individuality of the persons who enter into relation with each other (and not, as it were, into relation with something called 'the relation')?" (Kirkpatrick 1986: 64). Kirkpatrick worries that in such theories the "parts become less significant than the whole which includes them within itself" (Kirkpatrick 1986: 144).

Systems theories do not have to be read that way, however. A crucial term in systems theory is *boundary.* A well-functioning system contains sufficient boundaries around itself to maintain its coherence and integrity. A cell without a cell wall, or a relationship in which the members were as committed to others outside the relationship as to each other, would soon be swamped from the outside and not survive. A well-functioning system also contains sufficient boundaries around each individual component or member to preserve its individuality and differentiation. A cell that was only membranes would not be a cell at all. An authoritarian organization or a cult is a system that does not respect the personal boundaries of its members. In systems theory the category of boundaries carries the balance between individuality and interconnection. As long as the boundaries around the members are at least as strong as the boundaries tying the system together, systems do not have to be understood as subsuming the individual members into the collective.

The tone of the language here is rather different from Kirkpatrick's writing. The language of general systems theory—containing such categories as boundary, parts and wholes, and subsystems—is rather abstract when compared to Kirkpatrick's vivid and experience-near descriptions of divine and human agents and their actions. His language is obviously more compelling devotionally and closer to the speech of the sacred texts of, particularly, Western religion. But this does not necessarily mean that, on the more theoretical point of balancing autonomy and interconnection, his view is more balanced than that of systems theory. It may sound that way when systems models are confined to subhuman organic examples like cells. But systems theory has had a rich application in family therapy and organizational psychology (Hoffman 1981; Minuchin 1974). Despite their reliance on general systems theory, these disciplines treat individual persons as semi-autonomous agents capable of deliberation and action and not simply as cells in a larger organism.

As Kirkpatrick's writing illustrates, if we carry the image of relationship as a community of semi-autonomous interconnected agents into the realm of theology, the result is a concept of God as one personal agent "together bound" with other agents in a divine-human spiritual community. If we carry the systems image of relationships as systems of interconnected bounded members into the realm of religion, what might the result look like? It might look similar to Kirkpatrick's image of community. But, and this is what makes Kirkpatrick suspicious of systems theory, the theory does tend to emphasize the ontological priority or status of the larger system. Kirkpatrick wants to downplay the ontological status of the system or the relationship: persons enter into relationship with other persons rather than with some more encompassing whole. But this line of argument, in turn, sounds like Macmurray's mathematical, reductionistic thinking in which the relationship simply arises out of its parts. And the larger system can be afforded some ontological status without, as Kirkpatrick fears, going to the extent of subsuming the individual members into the larger system.

In a model of systems within systems, where do we locate the divine? Is God one part of the system or is God the larger system itself? If we locate God as one member of the system, we would bring the systems model more closely in line with Kirkpatrick's pluralistic image of divine-human community. If the term *divine* denotes the largest system as a whole, we bring the systems model closer to what Kirkpatrick calls monism. But one crucial difference remains. The image that emerges is not that of a great ocean absorbing all the component drops of water. Rather, the metaphysic is a system of interrelated but bounded, individuated, and semi-autonomous subsystems. This may be monism, but, if so, monism does not have to mean absorption.

On The Boundary of Psychoanalysis and Theology

Both psychoanalysis and theology have a role to play in the dialogue between them. Theological reflection, like that of Buber and Kirkpatrick, forces us to think more deeply about the structure of relationality, a reflection taking place at the interface of theology and contemporary psychoanalysis. Such interdisciplinary thinking carries the potential of deepening both fields. Contemporary psychoanalysis tells philosophers and theologians that all thinking is inherently relational. All theologies are relational theologies, whether that is acknowledged or not. Kohut points out that all human activities, including philosophy and theology, take place in a relational milieu. Winnicott sensitizes us to the ways in which philosophy and theology, like all cultural achievements, carry in their structures and categories echoes of our early relational themes and experiences (Jones 1992a).

In this dialogue, theology's role would be to take this psychoanalytic image of inherent relationality and carry it to its furthest reaches, thus connecting psychoanalysis and theology in a common exploration of human relationality and shedding light on the larger implications of a category that psychoanalysts may use unreflectively. The theologian might help the analyst see the larger implications of the analyst's implicit image of relationality. The analyst might help the theologian see the unconscious themes at work in the theologian's image of ultimate reality. Together they shed light on both the depths and heights of the human experience of existing as relational beings.

Religious thought often proceeds by taking a single aspect of human experience and making it a window on the transcendent: law in the case of Judaism and Islam, mathematics in Plato's philosophy, consciousness in certain schools of Hinduism and Buddhism. Contemporary theologians might begin from the experience of relationality (as Buber, Macmurray, and Kirkpatrick do), probing its extremes and extending it to include our relationship to our most ultimate and encompassing reality, whether that ultimate reality is a divine being, or the cosmos itself, or a spiritual presence immanent within the cosmos, or transcendental reality that includes the cosmos. However the sacred is named and described, we understand the ultimate by extrapolating from our deepest experience of interrelationship, whether that relationality is experienced monistically, dualistically, or pluralistically.

Theology shows us that whichever relational type is most congruent with our lived experience can be extended in order to generate our personal theological vision of our most ultimate relationship, or our relationship with what is most ultimate. Depending on our personal relational proclivities, we will come to know the ultimate as an undifferentiated cosmic source, or a transcendent divine power, or a personal being with whom we are bound together in love. In any case our theology will begin from our relational experience.

In this dialogue the role of psychoanalysis would be to shed light on the unconscious themes and dynamics involved in these three images of ultimate reality, which are also images of relationship. The monistic metaphysics, for example, are what Rolland referred to in his correspondence with Freud as an oceanic feeling. Freud interpreted this monistic experience as a regression to a pre-oedipal period of merger with the mother. Freud thought of the pre-oedipal phase as a time of mother-infant fusion, and in that context his claim that monistic experiences carry echoes of the earliest stage of development makes sense. More recent infancy research, however, has challenged Freud's view of development.

Daniel Stern, for example, in a book entitled *The Interpersonal World of the Infant* (1985), concludes that a rudimentary sense of self is present from birth. According to Stern, what is laid down in early childhood is not a series of developmental stages progressing from symbiosis to autonomy but, rather, sets of interpersonal interactions. For Stern the infant is interpersonal, rather than fused, from birth with an elementary capacity to initiate action, evoke responses in others, and respond to their responses. Entry into the world is entry into a reciprocal interpersonal field, and later development only enriches and complexifies what is there from the beginning.

For Stern, then, the "infant's life is so thoroughly social that most of the things the infant does, feels, and perceives occur in different kinds of relationships" (1985: 118). Even speech is considered important not primarily in terms of the cognitive capacity to transmit information but "in terms of forming shared experiences, of re-establishing the 'personal order,' of creating a new type of 'being-with'" (1985: 172). Rejecting the atomistic autonomy envisioned as the goal of child development (and treatment) in Freud's theory, Stern insists that the human life is fundamentally interpersonal from beginning to end.

Feeding an infant, putting an infant to bed, and changing diapers not only relieve physiological distress but the manner in which they are done also lays down certain interpersonal patterns and expectations. Such simple acts of child care are not only biological but also interpersonal. And the interpersonal lessons that the child learns from them persist long after the child has learned to feed and clothe himself or herself. According to Stern, these units of interaction generalize and become the building blocks of later interpersonal relations as well as the core sense of self. Shared affect (or lack of it) is fundamental to our earliest interpersonal experience. Stern suggests that "interaffectivity may be the first, most pervasive, and most immediately important form of sharing subjective experiences" (1985: 132). What he calls "affective attunement" is, he maintains, crucial in the development of a strong sense of self (1985: 138–161). This claim is similar to Kohut's theory of selfobject experience. (Stern's work and its import for the psychoanalysis of religion are discussed in more depth in Jones 1991a; for another example of a contemporary discussion of these developmental issues see Lichtenberg 1983.)

Given these findings, it is hard to maintain that monistic experiences represent a regression to a pre-oedipal period of fusion, as there is no pre-oedipal period of fusion. What dynamics are at work, then, in the monistic experience? Although more recent research has undermined the idea of a symbiotic developmental stage, this research does not explain why such an image struck such a responsive cord in Freud and countless later analysts who embraced the metaphor of infantile fusion. Perhaps it corresponded to something in their (and our) experience, even if it did not correspond to pre-oedipal existence. A potent image that is not necessarily grounded in reality is what Freud meant by an illusion. An illusion gains its appeal as the bearer of a wish. Perhaps the appeal of the metaphor of infantile symbiosis is that it carries a deep and abiding wish to merge and become completely one with another. Certainly such a wish is carried by much of the imagery of romance as well. The power of romance, and perhaps the power of monistic experience, derives not from a regression to a prior experience but from the wish for a future experience of joining. Thus there is no reason to call such a wish regressive. Rather, for whatever reasons of personal history, some among us (or perhaps all of us) may long to submerge our identities in something greater. Monistic mysticism and metaphysics may embody such a wish.

Likewise, the dualist's more distant relational metaphor carries certain unconscious themes. A gender-sensitive psychoanalysis reveals how science, philosophy, and religion express the desires of the unconscious, and how these desires may reflect the different developmental trajectories of boys and girls. Specifically Freud and much of modernity idealized that combination of investigation by detached observation, a motivation to dominate and control nature, and an atomistic and uncaring model of the universe, all of which serve as sublimations of the need for distance and separation that many have seen as endemic to masculine development. Men (and women, I might add) find such methods and images compelling to the extent that their character is fashioned around the same unconscious drive for distance.

When those same masculine dynamics (basic to modern science) are expressed religiously, they produce theologies of unmitigated transcendence. Again it is no coincidence that the religions of the modern era have been built on the *separation* of the human and the divine, the physical and the spiritual; and that such theologies arose in tandem with natural science, and that such theologies were uniformly composed by men. Whether the divine is represented by is the Deists' cosmic watchmaker, Descartes' sealing spirit off from matter, Kant's unknowable noumenon, Søren Kierkegaard's leap into the arms of the unknown, or Barth's deity chronically over-against the world, distance and separation—transcendence—has been its defining characteristic. Feminist analysis would suggest that, like the sciences of modernity, such theologies of transcendence (dualists, in Kirkpatrick's terms) appeal to those whose core conflict involves the need for separation.

What about the drive to overcome the dichotomy between fusion (carried by the monistic theologies) and distance (carried by dualistic theologies)? Such a drive is expressed by both Kirkpatrick's pluralistic theology and the systemic paradigm. What dynamics are at work here? This model of the self-in-relation corresponds to the model of selfhood found in contemporary relational psychoanalysis and modern infancy research. A theology that carries the image of the self as neither fused nor isolated is in line with the contemporary psychoanalytic understanding of selfhood. The image of the self-in-relation carries the twin longings for both affiliation and individuation that, according to Stern and others (for example, Lichtenberg 1983 and Mitchell 1988) are present throughout our lives. A theology that seeks to balance autonomy and interconnection may take a variety of forms, including the two examples previously discussed. To the extent that a person is inclined to stay close to concrete human relations, a theology like Kirkpatrick's theology of agent selves, including God, bound together in community may be compelling.

Feminist Theology

I see no reason why Kirkpatrick's pluralistic metaphor must be restricted to discussions of God as opposed to a Goddess. The image of the divine self in community with other selves seems resonant with many motifs of contemporary feminist theology and spirituality. One of the characteristics of many currents of feminist spirituality, especially those centering on the Goddess as an object of devotion, is the consistent personification of the divine. By making relationality the chief mode of divine existence, Kirkpatrick's discussion parallels the work of such feminist theorists as Gilligan, Miller, and Chodorow, who argue for the importance of relationality but claim that it is primarily a feminine trait. To the extent that they are correct in this, a thoroughly relational model of the divine would push theology in the direction of thealogy (Naomi Goldenberg's term for feminist religious reflection). A divine person whose primary mode of being is mutual relationship and connection sounds more like the image of the Goddess as portrayed in contemporary Goddess literature (Christ 1992; Eller 1993) than like the image of the masculine warrior and judge in the Hebrew Scriptures that was taken over into Christianity and Islam. (Further exploration of Goddess religion from both psychoanalytic and thealogical standpoints can be found in Jones and Goldenberg 1992.)

While rejecting the image of the Goddess, Sallie McFague, in her book *Models of God* (1988), argues for the theological use of feminine images for God. Like Kirkpatrick, she begins by insisting on an essentially personal and relational model of God. Personal language is the "richest model available to us" (1988: 82). While not exhausting God's nature, personal reality and therefore personal language represents the most complex and multidimensional reality we know and so is the most fitting language for divine reality. In addition, relationality demands personification. An unrelated God is religiously irrelevant, and a related God must be, in some sense, personal. Like Kirkpatrick and Macmurray, McFague wants to define the personal by the relational: to exist as a person is to exist in relation and to exist in relation is to exist as a person. For Kirkpatrick, Macmurray, and McFague, this statement applies to both human and divine realities.

If God is relational, what language should we use to describe and evoke that relationship? For McFague the traditional masculine language, drawn from the political realm, of God as lord, king, and judge connotes a relationship of dominance and submission, master and slave, rather than a mutual relationship of friendship and love. As Keller (1985, 1992) argued that modern Western science carries in its core the masculine image of power as domination and control, so McFague argues that what is glorified in the political metaphors for God's relation to the world is also masculine power as domination. Feminist theology goes beyond simply supplementing "he" with "she" or "father" with "mother" in theological and liturgical texts. What McFague and others are challenging are the deeper metaphors of relationship that have become central in Western theology and devotion. Even if God is called "she," what may be privileged is still a masculine image of relationship as power and control. Thus McFague wants to introduce into Western theology more intimate and interactive images of relationship. In our theological reflections and devotional disciplines, she suggests, we should experiment with images of God as mother, lover, and friend.

Kirkpatrick's and McFague's work illustrates one way in which theology is an inherently relational enterprise. Different models of God carry within themselves different images of relationship: monistic images of fusion, dualistic images of distance, pluralistic images of interaction, patriarchal images of dominion, maternal images of nurturance.

Process Theology

Another approach to the divine relationality can be found in the philosophy of Alfred North Whitehead. At the beginning of the twentieth century, Whitehead, who was a mathematician and physicist before he took up speculative philosophy, sought to construct a worldview that would harmonize science, philosophy and religion. He began from a vision, which he took from high-energy physics, of the interconnection of all events. The universe is a network of relationships in which each part is constituted by its interactions. Physics may speak of particles, but each particle is known only as a part of a larger, continually fluctuating pattern of particle interactions. These constant fluctuations at the quantum level mean that the apparently stable and solid ordinary physical world is, at its basis, continually in motion. Hence Whitehead's philosophy is often called "process philosophy" because everything in the cosmos is seen as continually in process. Whitehead (1929) himself called his system a "philosophy of organism" because he saw the interrelated world as a living organism rather than a dead machine.

For Whitehead every entity is connected through a web of relationships to every other. But every entity is also a unique individual because every event (events and entities are the same for Whitehead) incorporates all the past events that lead up to it. Whitehead is struggling here with the ancient philosophical problem of continuity and change. The chair I am sitting on, for example, has been repaired many times over the years I have had it. A leg was broken and I replaced it. The seat cracked and I bought an identical one. And the chair has been repainted several times. But I still think of it as the same chair (I am indebted to Frank Kirkpatrick for this example). On a deeper level, I am recognizably the same person at fifty that I was at ten, but little about me besides some basic physical characteristics is the same.

Both my continuity and that of the chair consist not in any formal attributes but in a continuity of experience in which past attributes are passed along and incorporated into the present moment of existence. The chair and I are both what we are right now because of what has happened to us in the past. And we will be what we are in the future because of what is happening to us right now and how that is incorporated and passed along. Each entity or event is both influenced by what came before and influences what comes after. Thus entities or events form an interconnected web of mutual interaction. Nothing, even God, exists independently. Everything is interconnected. To understand anything—a particle, a person, or an idea—is to see its relationship to everything around it and everything that preceded it. To understand is to see in context.

Although not formally religious, Whitehead was concerned to find a place for God in his system. God, according to Whitehead, has three primary characteristics or functions within the larger cosmic system. First, God is the source of order. God's purpose is the ultimate answer to the question of why the universe and its laws and structures have the form they do. Second, God is the source of novelty. God's creative action explains the emergence of new structures in the physical universe and new forms of evolutionary life. "Apart from God," Whitehead says, "there would be nothing new in the world, and no order in the world" (1929: 377). Third, as another entity (the supreme entity) in the larger cosmic system, God is reciprocally related to every other entity in the cosmos. God's purpose is eternal, but God too changes as "he" interacts with the rest of the cosmos, influencing the events in the universe and being influenced by them.

God's power is not, in Whitehead's schema, dictatorial or controlling. God does not overpower but persuades. He does not overrule but is one influence among others. God evokes responses; he is not a puppet master pulling strings. We are dependent on God, but God is also dependent on us to accomplish his goals. Not a transcendent dictator, God exists only in and through a loving reciprocal relationship with the universe. This leads the process theologians Cobb and Griffin (1976) to claim that Whitehead's metaphysics is the best expression of the claim that God is love.

Whitehead thus makes relationality the chief mode of divine existence, but in a way rather different from McFague, Macmurray, or Kirkpatrick. Kirkpatrick, drawing on Macmurray's categories, is critical of Whitehead's philosophy of organism (Kirkpatrick 1986: chap. 4). Like the organic philosophies Macmurray criticizes, Whitehead's system, according to Kirkpatrick, makes the whole—the web of interconnections—more basic and valuable than the parts—individual persons. For Macmurray and Kirkpatrick the individual actor is the primary unit of understanding; for Whitehead the primary unit is the system as a whole.

In part because his language in *Process and Reality* is so opaque, Whitehead's system strikes some readers as exceedingly abstract. He is forever coining new terms (which I have avoided in this brief exposition). In addition to his high level of generalization and his use of unfamiliar language, the abstraction of Whitehead's approach is also increased by his tendency to relate everything he discusses to the system as a whole. God, for example, exemplifies the principles of order, creativity, and interconnection and is understood as a part (the supreme part) of the larger cosmic system. Individuals, too, are "occasions" of interaction whose significance is derived from their contribution to the whole. Whitehead has made relationality, but not personhood, central. In Whitehead we have relations without persons.

Whether or not one finds Whitehead's metaphysical vision compelling, his system illustrates the emergence in the twentieth century of metaphors of relationship in a wide range of disciplines including natural science (or at least physics), philosophy, feminist theory, various schools of psychotherapy including psychoanalysis, and theology. Thus the dialogue between theology and psychoanalysis takes place in the context of a larger, cross-disciplinary convergence on the importance of relational paradigms.

Anthropomorphism Revisited

Two contrasting trends coexist within twentieth-century theology. Tillich, for example, insists that theology use the most universal language possible, a language shorn of all personal connotations. Personalistic language, Tillich feels, diminishes divine universality and reduces the absolute to the limits of finite personality. The image of a personal God is, for Tillich, a "confusing symbol," and it is better to speak of God in more universalizing terms as the "ground of being" or the "source of existence"

(Tillich's theology is discussed in more depth in Jones 1991a; see also Tillich 1951). Whitehead's philosophical theology, too, has a rather impersonal cast.

In contrast, Buber, Kirkpatrick, McFague, and Macmurray insist that only personal and interpersonal language is appropriate for God. Anything else makes God into an abstraction with whom no flesh-and-blood relationship is possible.

This tension is well known in the history of religions. Hinduism, for example, contains both the universalizing metaphysics of the Vedanta schools and radically personalistic devotional sects like the Hare Krishna movement. Buddhism has both the sparse universalism of Zen and the concrete particularity of the Japanese Pure Land groups.

At first glance, object relations theory, which champions interpersonal metaphors, would seem to support a more personalistic and anthropomorphic theology. If personal relations make us human, then theology (if it is not to be dehumanizing) must use primarily personal and relational language.

But we might make a distinction between a personal relationship and a relationship with a person. We have seen how, in different ways, Buber and Kohut insist that we may have a profoundly personal I-you or selfobject relationship with nature, or a book, or a piece of art or music. Every academic knows how abstract ideas can function as psychologically significant selfobjects (this point is discussed in more depth in relation to Tillich in Jones 1991a). Object relations theories privilege interactional and relational domains, but they do not necessarily insist that all relationships must be with persons. Thus it would be a mistake, I think, to argue that the theological use of object relations theory must point in the direction of radically personalistic and anthropomorphic theologies.

Besides, as Tillich himself recognized and insisted on, religious thought may use abstract conceptual language, but religious devotion demands the language of the personal deity (Tillich 1951, 1957). Prayers are rarely offered and hymns rarely sung to and rituals rarely centered on the "ground of being" or the ordering principle of the universe. Fervent prayer calls on the ten thousand Bodhisattvas on their diamond thrones, passionate hymns reach out to the Lord Jesus seated by the right hand of God, ecstatic ritual evokes the Great Mother in all her earthy presence. Such images are more personalistic and anthropomorphic but not necessarily more relational than the "emptiness" of philosophical Buddhism, the "pure existence" of Thomistic theology, or the "Brahma" of Upanishadic speculation.

In the history of religions both anthropomorphic images and conceptual categories play a part; the first is central to the experience of personal devotion, the second to the practice of philosophical reflection. All the world's great religions have contained both the ecstasies of ritual, trance, and fervent prayer and the logical rigors of philosophical speculation. Devotional ecstasy and metaphysical analysis are, respectively, the heart and head of the great traditions; together they form a whole and living religious organism.

Ever since Freud, psychoanalysis has been inclined to regard personalistic and anthropomorphic piety as infantile and primitive because there is a manifest connection between the language of devotional religion and the child's experience with its parents. Devotees are often called children or babies, and the deity is usually referred to as father or mother (for example, the Gospel of John centers on God the father, and Ramakrishna's spiritual autobiography centers on the divine mother). But from the standpoint of the history and phenomenology of religion, personalistic piety is not necessarily infantile or regressive. Anthropomorphic and philosophical forms of piety are just that, two different forms of religious experience and expression. One is not necessarily childish; rather, they serve different functions in the psychic economy of the tradition and the individual believer. In either case, religious expression takes place in a relational context: be it a theology embodying relational themes in abstract form and taking place in a relationship of devotion to philosophical analysis or an ecstatic relationship of devotion to a personal deity.

Relational theology need not be as radically personalistic as Buber, Macmurray, McFague, and Kirkpatrick imply. To the extent that a person is driven to go beyond concrete experience toward a more encompassing metaphysical vision or mystical experience, a modified monism will probably be attractive. Such transcendental states may be achieved through disciplined metaphysical speculation (for example, as described in the Upanishads or exemplified in the Buddhist dialectics of Nagarjuna or Tsongkhapa) or through various meditative practices (for example, Yogas of Hinduism or the Tantras of Tibetan Buddhism). But to the extent that such disciplines and practices grow from an image of the self-in-relation rather than the self as disappearing into the other, the result will be a transcendental experience of the self as both individuated and connected. Religious knowledge and experience, like all knowledge and experience, takes place in a relational context. If our religious practices, philosophical theologies, and devotional exercises take place in a context shaped by an experience of the self-in-relation, we will experience ourselves as individuated persons who stand in relation to the divine.

II

Knowing

5

Illusion

This book is organized around Freud's two approaches to the analysis of religion. The first part of this book—on human nature—concerns Freud's oedipal argument on the origin of religion in the creation of the superego out of the vicissitudes of the instincts. This second section—on human knowledge—follows from Freud's functional analysis of religion in terms of narcissism.

Narcissism and Knowledge

A central pillar of Freud's intellectual edifice was the "reality principle"—a metaphysical theory transformed into a diagnostic category. The "reality" behind the "reality principle" was the physical world as described by nineteenth-century physics. Armed with this clear and concise definition of what could be true and what had to be false, what could be real and what had to be imaginary, Freud was set up to attack religion as the product of irrationality and narcissism.

For Freud narcissism is the opposite of the reality principle and forms the earliest stage of development. The infant experiences himself or herself as omnipotent, the center of the universe. In the course of normal development, the inevitable intrusions of the reality principle frustrate this infantile grandiosity. The infant learns from encounters with reality to gradually renounce this feeling of omnipotence and accept the reality principle. Thus is narcissistic libido transformed into "object libido," in which the child comes to acknowledge the existence of reality in its own right and not to experience it as an extension of the infant's grandiosity.

Proper development journeys from primary process to secondary process, outgrowing the pleasure principle and embracing the reality principle. The illusory and the infantile are gradually brought under the control of the real and the rational. Any remaining infantile illusions are a continuation of a primitive mental state and so represent the greatest danger to rationality and sanity. Ways of knowing other than empirical science, the carrier of the reality principle, are not just logical errors or mistaken beliefs. They are psychopathologies.

If the reality principle is not sufficiently internalized, the person remains in the state of primitive narcissism. Such disparate phenomena as the delusions of the schizophrenic, the magical thinking of premodern cultures, and the blind idealization of romantic love are expressions of this infantile state. All involve what Freud calls overvaluation. The reality principle is subverted by the power of narcissistic wishes in which either the self or a beloved other is granted powers and qualities beyond what is realistic. Such illusions involve a retreat from reality into the seductively gratifying but ultimately destructive world of illusion.

Freud's argument depends on rigidly dichotomizing truth and fantasy, fact and fiction. Science embodies truth and fact; all else is fantasy and fiction—either the potentially useful fantasies found in art and literature or the potentially dangerous ones found in religion. Freud's monotheistic epistemology has no room for more than one route to the truth.

Within this framework Freud wrote his most sustained attack on religion, appropriately titled *The Future of an Illusion*. Illusions are defined by their appeal to narcissism. They are "not necessarily false," rather, "we call a belief an illusion when wish-fulfillment is a prominent factor" ([1927] 1964: 49). Thus Freud maintains that he is not discussing the truth value of religious beliefs but rather their psychological function, which is "that they are derived from human wishes" ([1927] 1964: 48).

Religion, he says, performs three functions, which all draw on infantile wishes. First, civilization is a dominant source of human misery because of its imposition of instinctual controls. Civilization inevitably leads to frustration. The rational person accepts this misery as the price paid for the advantages of culture. The immature person, however, demands to be rewarded in an imaginary heavenly realm of eternal, narcissistic bliss. Second, nature is impersonal, mechanical, uncaring. The adult accepts these facts of science and learns to live with the reality that his or her life, like all of nature, is meaningless and purposeless. The infantile flee from this harsh but realistic truth into the illusion that a caring and providential God stands behind the impersonal facade of nature. Third, from the first day of life fate continually deals harsh blows to human grandiosity. The greatest cruelty of fate is the finality of death. The realistic and rational person becomes resigned to life's capriciousness and transitoriness. The grandiose cannot accept that life is temporary and so cling to the illusion of life after death.

This understanding of religion makes sense only in the context of Freud's worldview. The idea, for example, that civilization opposes our natural instincts and so makes us miserable, and that this misery in turn requires a religious compensation, is not the only way to understand the relationship of society and the individual. If human beings are basically relational rather than antisocial (as Fairbairn and Macmurray argue), or if culture arises naturally out of psychological development (as Winnicott proposes), any inherent conflict between the psyche and society is considerably diminished. If the conflict is diminished, so is the necessity of this form of misery, and the theory that religion exists only to compensate for it is weakened.

Likewise with the impersonality of nature. Freud writes, "Nature rises up against us, majestic, cruel, and inexorable" ([1927] 1964: 21), unconcerned about our fate, "she" consists of "impersonal forces and destinies" ([1927] 1964: 22). Although not uncommon in the scientific circles of the nineteenth and twentieth centuries, this argument, many have commented, is a peculiar one (see, for example, Keller 1992: 117). Obviously it is a projection, a fact that Freud, with his astute sensitivities to others' projections, overlooks. Mary Midgley calls this argument the "drama of parental callousness" and writes, "There is the tone of personal aggrievement and disillusion, which seems to depend . . . on failure to get rid of the animism or personification which [these scientists] officially denounce. An inanimate universe cannot be hostile. . . . Only in a real, conscious human parent could uncaringness equal hostility. . . . [The universe is not] a callously indifferent human" (1985: 87; quoted in Keller

1992: 117). One can only wonder what in Freud's life is at the basis of such a projection.

In *The Future of an Illusion* Freud says that "assessing the truth value of religious doctrines does not lie within [his] scope" and acknowledges that not all wishes contradict reality ([1927] 1964: 52, 49). Yet, because "scientific work is the only road which can lead us to a knowledge of reality," Freud is driven beyond a functional analysis to a polemic that dismisses religion as an "all too palpable" contradiction to reason and experience" ([1927] 1964: 89). Religion, then, appeals to and reinforces our most infantile and narcissistic inclinations. It is culture's chief mode of denying reality. Religious claims cannot be "precipitates of experience or end results of thinking" but can only represent "fulfillments of the oldest, strongest, and most urgent wishes of mankind" ([1927] 1964: 47).

In spite of his methodological strictures about bracketing off the truth or falsity of religious claims, Freud's polemic against the antiscientific nature of religion breaks out time and time again in the midst of his discussion of the narcissistic roots of religion. This is not coincidence. Rather, the outbreak of this polemic alerts us to the possibility of a deeper connection between narcissism and the conflict of science versus religion. In the context of his discussion of science, Freud experiences religion as a threat and reacts with undisguised, if slightly unconscious, narcissistic fury.

Freud's discussion of narcissism brings together epistemology and psychopathology. Narcissism is not only a developmental stage or personality type, it is also an epistemological category. In Freud's view, narcissistic knowing is self-referred knowing. The infantile ego sees every event as an extension of its needs. The infant's lack of reality testing leads to the "omnipotence of thought" expressed as a belief in magic where thought makes physical reality conform to wish. In Freud's view narcissism is not only a threat to character development, it is also an assault on truth.

D. W. Winnicott

One of the major changes from classical theory has been a reappraisal of narcissism and primary process. Given the connection between narcissism and epistemology, this reappraisal signals a fundamental epistemological shift. Narcissism is no longer an infantile state to be outgrown but remains an abiding center of the personality. Rather than being the primary threat to sanity, narcissistic illusions are the source of creativity and culture.

D. W. Winnicott is the father of this revision. For him, the key to healthy development is not the imposition of the reality principle and the renouncing of illusion but just the reverse. The "facilitating environment" is so finely attuned to the infant's desires that the child learns to actualize, not suppress, his or her spontaneous wishes. If the reality principle is introduced too quickly, rather than mature rationality, the result is a compliant "false self" and loss of access to the spontaneous and creative "true self" within. For Winnicott the child must first consolidate a coherent sense of self made up of spontaneous desires and actions before confronting the harsh and unresponsive external world.

Gradually the child learns to accommodate external reality, facilitated by "transitional objects," which cushion the move from subjectivity to acknowledging the independence of the external world. These transitional objects (the proverbial blanket or teddy bear) both exist in the external world and are given their meaning and special status by the child's imagination. Thus they stand midway between the narcissistic world of the infant's experience and the reality-based world of the adult's.

Whereas Freud's demarcation of health and sickness is driven by a hard and fast distinction between reality and illusion, in *Playing and Reality* (1971) Winnicott moves beyond this dichotomy by proposing a "third area of human living, one neither inside the individual nor outside in the world of shared reality" (1971: 110). Between inner and outer lies *interaction*. Neither the objective environment nor the isolated individual but, rather, the interaction between them defines this third domain, for it "is a product of the *experiences of the individual* . . . in the environment" (107). This intermediate reality is interpersonal from its inception. Beginning in the interactional space between the mother and infant, it remains an interpersonal experience as it gradually spreads out from the relation to the mother to the "whole cultural field," for the "place where cultural experience is located is in the *potential space* between the individual and the environment (originally the object)" (1971: 100).

Key to the infant's move into the outside world is the use of the "transitional object," which "is not *inside*. . . . Nor is it *outside*" (1971: 41). Rather, it occupies that intermediate space that is interactional and thus carries for the infant the security of that first interpersonal experience (1971: 4). Playing with transitional objects is an essential part of the transitional process, for playing stands at the interface of the physical world and the world of inner psychological process. "This area of playing is not inner psychic reality. It is outside the individual, but it is not the external world. . . . Into this play area the child gathers objects or phenomena from external reality and uses these in the service of some sample derived from inner or personal reality. . . . . In playing, the child manipulates external phenomena in the service of the dream and invests chosen external phenomena with dream meaning and feeling" (1971: 51).

When playing, the child gives physical things an imaginative significance and enters a psychological space resonating with the earliest experiences of intimacy. Even when the baby plays alone, he or she is still operating interpersonally; the experience of play carries echoes of those first interactions, for the "playground is a potential space between the mother and the baby or joining mother and baby" (1971: 47). Thus Winnicott's theory is not primarily about certain kinds of objects—teddy bears and blankets—but about certain kinds of relational experiences.

Encompassing inner and outer reality, the transitional experience transcends the dichotomy of objectivity and subjectivity, for it is an "intermediate area of *experiencing*, to which inner reality and external life both contribute" (1971: 2). In Freud's positivistic epistemology, which rigidly dichotomized objectivity and subjectivity, there was no place for a way of knowing that was neither subjective or objective but contained elements of both. Thus Winnicott calls this transitional realm paradoxical. "In health the infant creates what is in fact lying around waiting to be found. . . . Yet the object must be found in order to be created. This has to be accepted as a paradox and not solved by a restatement that by its cleverness seems to eliminate the paradox" (1965: 181).

Heuristically we can separate subject and object, but, for Winnicott, they are, in actual experience, two sides of the same process. "Subject and object are inseparably interrelated as the human mind creates the object it finds. According to Winnicott, we create what exists, we create the objects of our environment, we create the other. And yet, paradoxically, the other also exists separately, apart from us. . . . For Winnicott external and internal reality are integrated, mutually influenced. What is external is simultaneously created by the individual" (Jonte-Pace 1985: 230).

The world of the infant's experience (and our own adult world) is both created and found, constructed and discovered. We are neither the passive recipients of brute facts imposed on us from outside nor (in health) do we make our own realities out of nothing. Human knowing is an active, creative process (Jones 1989) in which reality is simultaneously discovered and constructed.

Knowledge occurs in and through a relationship: our relationship to the world which we both find and create. Knowledge arises not from the self alone nor from the world alone but from the interaction between them. Winnicott's focus is on the transitional process as *interaction*. Occurring in a relational space between self and world, subject and object, human knowing is a transitional process. Like all transitional processes, that interactional and relational space that is human understanding echoes with the child's first interpersonal experiences. This makes possible the psychoanalysis of the various forms of human knowledge (science, art, religion, philosophy, even psychoanalysis itself), for the structures of our knowing carry themes laid down in our earliest interpersonal encounters.

Psychoanalysis is an inherently epistemological enterprise, laying bare the relational dynamics at work in the various forms of human knowing. Natural science, religious experience, novels and symphonies outwardly express unconscious themes that, contemporary psychoanalysis suggests, enter the unconscious through the internalization of interpersonal experiences. We are attracted to empiricism's drive for objectivity and control, or Islam's insistence on moral purity, or the paradoxical logic of Zen, or the vision of human nature as the competition of selfish genes, or Béla Bartók's clashing chords in part because they resonate with the structures of our personality that are the result of early relational events.

Hans Loewald

For Freud the id was the realm of blind, self-centered, instinctual chaos—the continuing potential for regression and neurosis within the individual. Narcissism meant never outgrowing the id's infantile fantasies and wishes. The development of the ego carried the hope of gaining some rational control over it—"where id is, let ego be." Freud's was the Stoic's hope of rational self-mastery and resignation. The worst fate was to fall prey to the blind, irrational forces within.

For Hans Loewald, the id, the unconscious, is not simply the cause of neurosis. As the source of reason, it has a rationality all its own, for the "undifferentiating unconscious is a genuine mode of mentation which underlies and unfolds into a secondary process mentation (and remains extant together with it, although concealed by it)" (1978: 64–65).

Different spheres of mental activity are created from, and should remain in contact with, their primary source in the id. Both aspects of this dialectic are essential. Higher mental processes are established out of our instinctual nature. But our "primary processes" must also remain available to us. As opposed to Freud's attempt to keep id and ego, instinct and reason, in hermetically sealed compartments so that the purity of reason would not be contaminated by the irrationality of instinct, Loewald writes:

> There is no one way street from id to ego. Not only do irrational forces overtake us again and again; in trying to lose them we would be lost. The id, the unconscious modes and contents of human experience, should remain available. If they are in danger of being unavailable—no matter what state of perfection our 'intellect' may have reached—or if there is a danger of no longer responding to them . . . [we must find] a way back to them so they can be transformed, and away from a frozen ego. (1978: 22)

Such returns to primary processes are sources of creativity and refreshment. Discursive reason alone renders human life sterile, unless reason has access to the more unitive and intuitive forms of knowing grounded in the unconscious.

The range and richness of human life is directly proportional to the mutual responsiveness between these various mental phases and levels. . . . [Rational thought] limits and impoverishes . . . the perspective, understanding, and range of human action, feeling, and thought, unless it is brought back into coordination and communication with those modes of experience that remain their living source, and perhaps their ultimate destination. It is not a foregone conclusion that man's objectifying mentation is, or should be, an ultimate end rather than a component and intermediate phase. (1978: 61)

Primary processes, with their complementary forms of rationality, should be accessible to even the most highly developed intellect. Sanity consists not in renouncing primary process but in remaining open to it.

Loewald's discussion clearly parallels Winnicott's desire to break through the dichotomy between objectivity and subjectivity, but Loewald rejects Winnicott's contention that the infant moves from subjectivity to objectivity, aided by transitional objects. For Loewald (1988: 78–79), the infant's experience exists before the differentiation of objectivity and subjectivity and represents an awareness that embraces both. Our consciousness of ourselves (which we usually call subjectivity) and our consciousness of objects (which we usually call objectivity) are both states of consciousness. Objectivity does not mean a lack of human awareness but a particular form of human awareness—one focused on the "not self." In objectivity the contents of my awareness do not belong to me (they are objects in the world of space and time), but my *awareness* of them still belongs to me and is, in that sense, subjective. Objectivity is not opposed to "subjectivity" (understood as human awareness) but is, rather, one form of it. Thus the attempt to create an "objective" psychoanalysis is inevitably doomed, for psychoanalysis is in fact "in the forefront of efforts to break the hegemony of the modern scientific *natura naturata* interpretation of reality" (1988: 79).

Although Loewald casts his argument as a response to Winnicott, he does not apply his conception of a wider subjectivity to a reformation of Winnicott's idea of transitional phenomena except to say that he suspects that "Winnicott would not have disagreed with an interpretation of subjectivity in a wider and different sense, as outlined here" (1988: 80). If, however, no linear movement takes place from id to ego, from subjectivity to objectivity, but instead a reciprocal movement goes on between them, and if a wider subjectivity embraces what we call both objectivity and subjectivity, then such terms as *objectivity, subjectivity,* and *transitional phenomena* do not refer to rigidly separate realities. Rather, they refer to differing permutations of human consciousness, different states along a continuum of awareness (Jones 1992).

Implicit in the statements of both Winnicott and Loewald is a different view of childhood from that of Freud. Freud considered development in a linear way: childhood, narcissism, illusion, and primary process must all be outgrown in the name of that autonomous rationality that is the crowning achievement of adulthood. For Winnicott and Loewald (who writes, "To be an adult . . . does not mean leaving the child in us behind" [1978: 21–22]), creativity, not discursive rationality alone, is essential to the fully human life. Childhood imagination and spontaneity are reappropriated positively by Winnicott and Loewald as the sources of creativity rather than disowned as a threat to rational objectivity. The transitional process represents a comprehensive view of human nature that values creativity, spontaneity, imagination, and intuition along with critical reason and autonomous action.

The transitional process forms a state of consciousness or psychological space for which Winnicott uses the term *illusion,* thereby converting the term from a synonym for error into a source of truth by making it synonymous with creativity and insight. The creative intuition fostered in the transitional space is a crucial human mode of knowing. W. W. Meissner writes of Winnicott, in words that could equally apply to Loewald:

> Illusion in this view is not an obstruction to experiencing reality but a vehicle for gaining access to it. If Freud wished to rule out illusion and destroy it, Winnicott wished to foster it and to increase man's capacity for creatively experiencing it. Winnicott sees that illusion is an important part of human experience precisely because it is not by bread alone that man lives. Man needs to create,

to shape and transform his environment, find vehicles for expressing his inner life, or rather the constant commerce between the ongoing worlds of his external experience and his inner psychic reality. Winnicott's standard of psychic health is not the separation of the real and the wishful, as Freud might have had it, but rather their constant intermingling and exchange. It is through illusion, then, that the human spirit is nourished. (1984: 177)

Playing with reality is not only for psychological relief, it provides the perspectives that nurture creativity in the arts and sciences.

Loewald and Winnicott underscore the creative power of that state of consciousness where the usual distinctions of inner and outer, subjective and objective, fade and what Loewald refers to as a "deeper level of mentation" (1978: 61) is accessed: a creative power that can be understood in terms of the metaphorical nature of all human knowledge. In this state of disciplined imagination or what the theologian Paul Tillich calls "ecstatic reason," new metaphors and paradigms can be encountered. From the transforming interpretation that reframes a patient's experience to Watson's dream of the DNA spiral to the imaginative encounter with the holy, transitional experiences become epistemically creative and psychologically restorative through the generation of new metaphors and therefore new realities.

Knowledge in Transition

In his drive to go beyond the dualism of objectivity and subjectivity that has dominated not only psychology but all modern culture (Jones 1982), Winnicott carries into psychoanalysis a theme central to much current philosophy of science (Jones 1981) and to other contemporary movements. His search for the "intermediate area between the subjective and that which is objectively perceived" (Winnicott 1971: 3) is clearly part of a larger cultural concern (Jones 1982).

Richard Bernstein (1983), for example, in a book whose title, *Beyond Objectivism and Relativism,* summarizes its intent, chronicles a transformation in our understanding of science since Freud (a discussion of these changes can be found in Jones 1981). Drawing on the writings of such contemporary philosophers of science as Paul Feyerabend, Richard Rorty, and especially Thomas Kuhn, he describes a "shift from a model of rationality that searches for determinate rules . . . to a model of practical rationality that emphasizes the role of . . . interpretation. . . . The real point is to show what is wrong with a theory or understanding of the 'cognitive' which restricts this honorific term to what can be explicitly formulated in a series of propositions" (1983: 57). Bernstein demonstrates that the supposedly inviolate dichotomy between objectivity and subjectivity, reason and emotion, depends on an indefensibly narrow restriction of rationality to rule-governed procedures (such as laboratory science and math). This, in turn, relegates everything else to the intellectual hinterland of subjectivity.

A careful analysis of the actual conduct of science reveals that "many traditional or standard theories of what constitutes the rationality of science are inadequate and need to be revised if we are to make sense of how science functions and in what sense it is a rational activity" (Bernstein 1983: 59). Instead of the usual empiricist model of reason as a set of universal rules, scientific rationality (and by extension reason in general) requires "imagination, interpretation, the weighing of alternatives, and application of criteria that are essentially open" (1983: 56). Bernstein proposes replacing the strict model of rationality, which undergirded the modern ideal of knowledge, with a "practical rationality" (1983: 230). The merits of this suggestion are less important for our purposes than his demonstration of how a more contemporary and nuanced view of science challenges the dichotomy that Freud assumed and built into the structure of his theories, including his metapsychology.

Similarly, Nelson Goodman, in *Of Mind and Other Matters,* insists that all cognitive activities, especially "knowing, acting, and understanding in the arts, sciences, and life in general involves the use—the interpretation, application, invention, revision—of symbol systems" (1984: 152). Art and science share a "common cognitive function," and both can be "embraced within epistemology conceived as the philosophy of understanding. . . . Since science and art consist very largely in the processing of symbols" (1984: 146).

Goodman insists that we have no "self-evident truths, absolute axioms, unlimited warranties to distinguish right from among coherent
versions" (1984: 37). Bernstein's response is to rely on pragmatic criteria
and accept those claims that are proven in practice. Goodman proposes
a radically pluralistic viewpoint in which there can be many separate "versions . . . true in different worlds" (1984: 31).

Bernstein builds his epistemology from materials provided by the history and philosophy of science. Lakoff and Johnson, in *Metaphors We
Live By* (1980), arrive at similar conclusions from an analysis of how
claims are linguistically embedded. Claims to knowledge are systems of
language. This linguistic inevitability means we have no unmediated access to reality. Theory and data cannot finally be separated—we wouldn't
even know what counts for data except in the presence of some theory
(Jones 1981). The characteristics we attribute to objects in our world "exist and can only be experienced relative to a conceptual system" (Lakoff
and Johnson 1980: 154).

Empiricist views of knowledge depend on a correspondence theory
of truth: statements are called true when they correspond to some outside reality. The mediated nature of knowledge marks the end of any such
theory, for we have no direct access to that external reality against which
to compare our claims. There are no claims without contexts, and eval-
uation is a process conducted within some conceptual network.

Lakoff and Johnson call these basic conceptual networks "metaphors":
scientific discourse may depend on a metaphor of causation as a kind of
action; business decisions may be made by envisioning labor as a kind of
resource; relationships may be conducted under the rubric of love as a
journey; and intellectual discussion may be governed by the metaphor
of argument as war. Metaphor "pervades our conceptual system and is a
primary mechanism for understanding" (1980: 196).

Our reality—that is, the world of our lived experience—is shaped by
the metaphors through which experience is mediated, and so it is no exaggeration to say that metaphors "create realities" (1980: 156). This is because "we define our reality in terms of metaphors and then proceed to
act on the basis of the metaphors. We draw inferences, set goals, make
commitments and execute plans, all on the basis of how we in part struc-

ture our experience, consciously or not, by means of metaphor" (1980: 158). The function of metaphor is precisely to "highlight and make coherent certain aspects of our experience . . . [and] be a guide for future action. Such actions will, of course, fit the metaphor. This will, in turn, reinforce the power of the metaphor to make experience coherent" (1980: 156).

The empiricist ideal of objectivity was based on the metaphor of truth as correspondence. Given the dichotomous nature of modern thought, undermining the myth of correspondence seems to leave only subjectivity. To argue for a contextual epistemology is to confront the charge of subjectivism (for example, see Kuhn's "Postscript—1969" in Kuhn 1972; and Jones 1981, chap. 5). Lakoff and Johnson, like Bernstein and Winnicott, respond by pushing us past this dualism: "The mistaken cultural assumption [is] that the only alternative to objectivism is radical subjectivity—that is, either you believe in absolute truth or you can make the world in your own image. If you're not being objective, you're being subjective, and there is no third choice. We see ourselves as offering a third choice to myths of objectivism and subjectivism" (1980: 185).

They call their third alternative *experientialism.* Knowledge arises neither from the external world impressing itself on our passive minds or from the projection of our subjective ideas onto a blank screen. Instead "we understand the world through our interactions with it" (1980: 194). Like Winnicott's transitional process, such a philosophy is neither subjective nor objective but a third alternative. Write Lakoff and Johnson:

> Its emphasis on interaction and interactional properties shows how meaning always is meaning to a person. . . . it gives an account of how understanding uses the primary resources of the imagination via metaphor and how it is possible to give experience new meaning and to create new realities. . . . we see the experientialist myth as capable of satisfying the real and reasonable concerns that have motivated the myths of both subjectivism and objectivism but without either the objectivist obsession with absolute truth or the subjectivist insistence that imagination is totally unrestricted. (1980: 228)

Perhaps a better name for their proposal (in keeping with Winnicott's terminology) would be an "interactionalist epistemology," as "understanding emerges from interaction, from constant negotiation with the environment and other people. . . . From the experientialist perspective, truth depends on understanding, which emerges from functioning in the world" (1980: 230). Or, in Winnicott's more vivid language, truth is both "created and found." Such an account, Lakoff and Johnson say, "meets the objectivist's need for an account of truth . . . [and] satisfies the subjectivist's need for personal meaning and significance" (1980: 230).

Metaphors stand conceptually between objectivity and subjectivity, involving discursive reason and creative expression. Metaphor is thus a transitional phenomenon. Our most rule-governed activities, like experimental method, depend for their construction, elaboration, and expression on metaphors that "unite reason and imagination" (Lakoff and Johnson 1980: 193). Rizzuto, in the spirit of Winnicott and Meissner, writes, "In ordinary language . . . illusory and real are antithetical, mutually exclusive concepts. This is not so in the private realm of transitional reality where illusory and real dimensions of experience interpenetrate each other to such an extent that they cannot be teased apart without destroying what is essential in the experience" (1979: 227). Lakoff and Johnson suggest that this is not only true of the inner world but is equally true of the worlds of science, culture, and critical philosophy, for all "human conceptual systems are metaphorical in nature and involve an imaginative understanding" (1980: 194).

Another argument for the metaphorical nature of human knowledge can be found in a book written jointly by a cognitive psychologist and a philosopher of science. Michael Arbib and Mary Hesse, in *The Construction of Reality* (1986), insist that "all language is metaphorical" (150) and apply this maxim to psychology, religion, and the philosophy of science. "The rise of science was accompanied by the conception of an 'ideal language' that would enable us to read off from the 'book of nature' the true science that exactly expresses reality" (Arbib and Hesse 1986: 149). Empiricism requires an "ideal, universal language exactly matching the world" (1986: 158). But a careful analysis of language leads them to reject the empiricist's "view of language as an ideal static system with fixed meanings which are dependent upon . . . rules" (1986: 148). Rather, language systems in the sciences and humanities are a "complex web of semantic interactions in which there is no rigid distinction between the literal and the metaphorical" (1986: 146). Changes in scientific theory or movement from the sciences to the humanities involves primarily a change in categories. New theories in science or scientific and artistic models achieve a "metaphoric redescription" of experience (1986: 156).

Inevitably a view of knowledge as mediated (rather than passively imprinted on our brains) leads them to an interactional model of human knowing. "There is an essential interaction between the knowing subject and the world, both in terms of the linguistic categories brought to the world in describing it, and in the activity of the subject in physical relations with the world" (1986: 159). Here the philosopher's concern with metaphor dovetails with the psychologist's theory of cognitive schema. "Schema theory interprets human perception, action, and communication in terms of cognitive schemas. . . . these schemas change with experience. They do not reflect the full meaning of external reality but are always (at least potentially) in a state of flux, subject to change through our dialogue with the world" (1986: 181). Only through cognitive, linguistic categories do we understand the world of our experience. The furthest reaches of scientific theorizing belong to the domain of human creativity, for even "scientific theory provides constructed models of scientific reality" (159).

Winnicott struggled to move beyond Freud's nineteenth-century dichotomy of reason and imagination, objectivity and subjectivity, by the articulation of a third, or transitional, realm, rooted in interpersonal experience. Contemporary philosophy of science, as summarized by Arbib and Hesse, converges with Winnicott's concern to transcend these dualisms and reinstate imaginative interaction as a source of knowledge: "Scientific models are a prototype . . . for imaginative creations or schemas. . . . Symbolic worlds all share with scientific models the function of describing and redescribing the world; and for all of them it is inappropriate to ask for literal truth as direct correspondence with the world. . . . We do not suddenly put on a different hat with regard to 'truth' when we speak of the good or God from that we wear for natural science" (1986: 161). Arbib and Hesse go on to make an implication of special relevance to controversies in contemporary psychoanalysis—"there is little difference in principle here between the human and the natural sciences" (1986: 177).

Whereas Freud and many contemporary positivists think in terms of a strict dichotomy of reason and imagination, a more nuanced philosophy of science concurs that all knowledge is transitional and interactional in Winnicott's sense. Discursive reason and imaginative creation interpenetrate. Pragmatic realities constrain imaginative reconstructions, while creative reinterpretations reframe empirical experience. No precise line can be drawn between objective and subjective spheres or between the products of reason and of imagination. This applies to psychoanalysis, molecular genetics, and the philosophy of religion (Jones 1981).

6

The Dilemmas of Reductionism

When psychology and religion approach each other, the problem of reductionism always seems close at hand. Can psychoanalysis investigate religion without reducing religion to a purely psychological phenomenon?

Freud exemplifies the reductionistic interpretation of religion. In his oedipal analysis of religion, Freud makes three rather different types of claims. First, Freud describes the psychodynamics of religion, implying that unconscious processes are involved in all types of religious experience, that "religion, morality, and a social sense—the chief elements in the higher side of man—are acquired phylogenetically out of the father complex" ([1923] 1960: 34). Second, he asserts that this psychodynamic account is a complete account, "that at bottom God is nothing other than an exalted father" ([1913] 1950: 147). And third, Freud maintains that all religious statements can be reduced to statements about psychological processes, that statements about our "higher nature" really refer to "our relation to our parents" ([1923] 1960: 32).

Although these three claims are often seen as variations on the same theme, they are far from equally compelling. The first seems to me indisputable and is the sine qua non of any psychoanalytic investigation of religion. One can agree that psychological processes are implicated in religious experience without accepting Freud's account of them. But this raises the question whether it is possible to describe these psychological dynamics and also affirm that more is involved in religious experience than simply psychological factors. Can psychoanalysts analyze religion *and* maintain that religion is not simply a subsystem of psychology, as

Feuerbach and Freud thought? Is it rational to believe that a religious account of life is not simply redundant but that it adds insights beyond those provided by psychology?

The psychoanalysis of religion simply assumes that religious experience, like all human experience, is psychological in nature. That is, it is mediated through our cognitive and neuronal systems; it compels us because of motivational factors in our personality; it has unique elements for each individual because of each individual's unique personal history. That same could be said of the experience of conducting a scientific experiment, listening to a symphony, or engaging in sex. To say that there are cognitive, neuronal, motivational, and psychodynamic aspects to a religious experience no more negates its being a *religious* experience than those factors negate a scientific discovery's being scientific.

Freud's second and third claims, in contrast, are highly problematic and unconvincing. These claims constitute Freud's reductionistic account of religion.

The Nonlogic of Reductionism

Such reductionism was common in the Newtonian science of Freud's day, in which the goal was to reduce all statements about events in the ordinary world to what Clark Maxwell called "matter in motion." Since the late nineteenth century, several problems have been found with that reductionistic program even within the physical and biological sciences. I will mention three.

SYSTEMS PROPERTIES

Modern science often portrays the cosmos as a series of interconnected but relatively autonomous levels (Bohm 1957; Jones 1984). Specific properties characterize specific levels. A metal has color, texture, and strength; the individual molecules that make it up do not. The molecules have bonding properties that atoms lack. The particles that make up the atoms have virtually none of the properties associated with the objects of our ordinary experience. They lack density, color, and (in some cases) mass or extension in space and time. Descriptions of, say, color cannot be reduced to statements about protons; color is a property of substances, not of individual particles.

To give another example, physics provides a complete account of the processes of ionization, how filaments give off positive and negative ions whose wave properties create red and blue colors. With all that physics in hand, we still can't tell that those ions make a sign that says "Joe's Bar and Grill" or what that means to a hungry traveler. And no theory of ionization could possibly help us understand the meaning of that sign. No theory of molecular bonding and the constitution of metal will provide a clue to the nature of an automobile engine. Although the sign is clearly made of ions and the engine made of particles, atoms, and molecules, neither the meaning of the sign nor the nature and function of an engine can be reduced to statements about elementary particles, atoms, or molecules. The meaning of the sign and the function of the motor are properties of the system, not of the individual components.

Therefore, while some physical phenomena can be completely analyzed in terms of their component parts, that has not proven true of all phenomena. Some phenomena display properties that might be referred to as "systems properties"—properties that cannot be totally accounted for in terms of an analysis of component parts. Likewise, one might claim that religious experience is made up of psychological processes without also maintaining that statements about God, or the moral life, or the immortality of the human spirit can be reduced to statements about oedipal conflicts or internalized object relations. One might claim that religious experiences, as well as, say, an appreciation of the music of Bach, or the joy of scientific research, have properties that cannot be completely accounted for in psychodynamic terms.

THE LOGIC OF REDUCTIONISM

Strictly speaking, to reduce one set of statements to another implies that the first set is logically entailed by the second and that therefore we ought to be able to predict the first from the second. So, for example, we can predict the gravitational attraction of two bodies if we know their mass and distance apart by use of Newton's inverse square law.

Logically, if one set of statements can be reduced to a second set of statements (for example, if statements about living cells can be reduced to statements about the chemicals that make up those cells), the properties described by the first set of statements should be strictly predictable from the properties described by the second set of statements. In other words, I ought to be able to predict the characteristics of living cells from a description of chemical compounds. This has proven impossible in most cases. Usually we know in advance the properties of the first set when we come to study the second. So when we investigate the second, we automatically concentrate on the properties of the second class of statements that strike us as most similar to the first set. We connect the properties of the chemical hydrogen, for example, to the structure of the hydrogen atom. But we knew in advance the properties of hydrogen, which certainly helped us explain them on the basis of the structure of the hydrogen atom. It is not clear that we would be able to predict in advance the nature of hydrogen if all we had was a single hydrogen atom.

Freud thought that the relationship between manifest and latent content, between conscious content and unconscious dynamic, was the same as the relationship between ordinary objects and the atoms that constitute them. Just as forces and structures at the atomic level often determine the nature of ordinary objects, so, for Freud, forces at the unconscious level determine the contents of consciousness. Freud spoke of this in the decidedly Newtonian terms of psychic determinism, which was certainly in keeping with the science of Freud's day.

Although deterministic relations hold between the atomic and the molecular levels, other relationships exist within nature that are not necessarily deterministic. At the subatomic level, for example, there is randomness and indeterminacy. Events at this level are often expressed in a probability calculus rather than deterministically. Events at the subatomic, atomic, and ordinary levels are connected but not always in the deterministic way that strict reductionism requires. This is what it means to say that the various levels or domains that make up the cosmos are semi-autonomous (Bohm 1957; Jones 1984).

Likewise, we can affirm that unconscious forces are at work in religion (as well as in art, literature, and science) and draw connections between, say, ideas of God and oedipal conflicts or interpretations of sacred stories and selfobject needs without necessarily claiming that one set of statements can be reduced to the other. One can assert that a connection exists between religious beliefs and psychodynamic processes, but it is not clear that we could predict the whole kaleidoscope of religious phenomena just from studying parent-child interactions in the way that the logic of strict reductionism would require.

The Nature of Theory

Science is made of theories. The reductions that are possible at any given time are a function of the state of our theories and what connections can be made between groups of theories. The laws of thermodynamics, for example, can be derived from the kinetic theory of molecular motion when temperature at the thermodynamic level is equated with kinetic molecular motion. Technically temperature refers to the macro-level and has no meaning at the molecular level: gases have temperature, molecules do not.

By their nature, theories are selective (Jones 1986, 1981). In the face of complex phenomena, natural science selects some aspects as relevant for its purposes and brackets out others. Take the common physical problem of falling bodies: a weight released from a tower, a man jumping from a building, and a rock falling from a ledge are all falling bodies. From the standpoint of physics all are the same. All can be subsumed under the same mathematical formula, which describes the fall of objects to the earth. This general rate of descent, the only thing that interests the physicist as physicist, is obviously not the only important dimension. If you are the wife or child of the man who jumped from the building, or if you are struck by the rock that topples from the ledge, calculating the rate of descent will not be the first thing on your mind. Science selects some aspects of experience (in this case the rate of descent) as relevant and ignores all others: the excitement of the experimenter, the grief of the suicide victim's family, the pain of skull fracture.

This selectivity is guided by pragmatic concerns. All theories concentrate only on those aspects of experience that are relevant for their task, such as the task of giving a mathematical account of motion. The meaning of a theory, then, is related to the use to which it is put. Its meaning is its function within a specialized discipline (Toulmin 1985).

Theories are like maps. We have different maps for different purposes: a road map to guide our motoring, a geological map to help us find mineral formations, a map of climatic conditions, another of political boundaries, and so on. Each map has a different function, and we must choose the right one for the right purpose: motoring, hiking, surveying, mining. Different maps are different ways of representing phenomena for different purposes. The same is true of different theories (Toulmin 1985).

Thus a single phenomenon can be viewed in a variety of equally valid ways. Take a painting, for example. If I ask an art historian, a professor of aesthetics, a chemist, and a gallery owner about the value of the painting, I'll get several different answers. The art historian will tell me of its place in the history of art. The professor of aesthetics will speak of its symmetry and balance. The chemist will describe the makeup of the pigments. The gallery owner will give me its current dollar value. Each account serves a different purpose, answers a different question, and so focuses on a different aspect of the painting. If I want to know why the color has faded, I ask the chemist and not the aesthetics professor. If I want to know why the painting is considered important enough to be in a museum, I ask the art historian and not the chemist. If I want to know why it's so expensive, I ask the gallery owner, and so on.

Selectivity and the different uses of theory mean that every account is necessarily incomplete. There is no single account of a phenomenon. As we can envision different accounts of one painting, we can imagine different accounts of religious experience in terms of different disciplinary goals and functions. An analytic account of the psychological processes that go into a religious experience no more negates a theological account than a description of the chemistry of pigments necessarily negates an analysis of the aesthetics of a painting.

Absolute and Heuristic Reductionism

The limited nature of all human theories creates a distinction between what we might call "absolute" and "heuristic" reductionism. Absolute reductionism is the metaphysical claim that, in reality, all subsequent phenomena are determined by and completely explicable in terms of lower-level processes. We have seen that this Newtonian assumption, which defined science in Freud's day, has serious logical and empirical problems. When Freud declares that "God is nothing but an exalted father figure," he is being absolutely reductionistic in this sense. Thus he transforms the psychoanalysis of religion into the religion of psychoanalysis—that is, he maintains that psychoanalysis provides the only complete account of all human behavior.

Heuristic reductionism, in contrast, seeks to understand one field in terms of another. Examples include studying biological systems in terms of chemical properties, or studying human behavior in terms of genetic reproduction, or studying religious experiences in terms of psychological processes. Such procedures do not entail that biological processes are just chemistry or that human behavior is only genetic replication or that religious experiences are just psychology. Within the limits of a discipline they may be treated that way for purposes of study. But, given the inherent incompleteness in all disciplines, such single accounts cannot be the whole story.

When we say that a certain account is incomplete or inadequate, we must ask for what purpose it is incomplete or inadequate. To answer the question of why the paintings of Michelangelo have faded over time, a chemical account is sufficient. To answer the question of why such paintings should be preserved at great cost, a discussion of chemical substances is not adequate. If we want to find mineral deposits in upstate New York, a geological survey map of the area will be sufficient. If we want to survey for political boundaries, such a map will be woefully inadequate. If we want to know why Albert Einstein was attracted to mathematical physics, a good psychobiographical account will surely help us. If we want to know if the theory of general relativity is complete, an account of Einstein's childhood will be irrelevant. Likewise, if we want to know why Martin Luther's or Jiddu Krishnamurti's religious experiences took the form they did, psychoanalytic accounts like those provided by Erik Erikson or Sudhir Kakar are useful. But if we want to know if life has a purpose or if forgiveness triumphs over death, the psychoanalysis of religious experience is no substitute for religious experience.

Like the methodological atheism of the physical sciences, a *methodological* reductionism is inherent in social scientific research into religion, which, of necessity, treats religious belief and practice as the dependent variable and psychological processes as the independent variable. But this heuristic reductionism is a function of the chosen method and does not logically entail a reductionism in reality. To argue that social scientific research demonstrates that religion is only a psychological process is to argue in a circle and mistake method for conclusion. Such reductionism is also predicated on an outmoded understanding of the relationship of theory and data and on a mechanistic model of nature which has been repudiated in the physical sciences.

Parts, Wholes, and Hierarchies

Arguing against reductionism on the basis of the necessary incompleteness in any theoretical account portrays the various disciplines as a series of heuristically self-contained compartments (Jones 1981). Each develops its own methods and theories around the core questions it seeks to answer, the particular problems it seeks to solve, and goals it wishes to achieve. Such a model emphasizes discontinuity between disciplines, advocates a pluralistic and pragmatic approach to human understanding, and exemplifies a compartmentalized view of the relationship among disciplines.

The various disciplines can, however, also be seen as a series of more encompassing sets, fitting within each other like larger and larger containers. Natural processes at certain levels of complexity, for example, cannot be completely described in language of their component parts. Describing biological processes necessitates terms not required to explain simple chemical reactions: *hierarchy, organization, structure,* and even *information* become important constructs for describing living systems. The result is a hierarchy of theories, of descriptions, each more encompassing and each introducing novel concepts.

A simple analogy is the relation of letters, sentences, and a book. A book is made up of sentences, sentences are made up of words, and words are made up of letters. A book is not just a random assortment of letters.

The selection of letters in a book is a function of the words in a book. The selection of words in a book is a function of sentences in a book. The selection of sentences in a book is a function of the overall theme of the book. In this hierarchy the whole governs the parts as much as the parts govern the whole. The order of letters in a book cannot be explained just by looking at letters or even words. Nor can I give a complete account of the theme of the book solely in terms of the structure of individual letters or words. Contrary to the reductionistic account, which sees the whole only in terms of the parts, explaining the structure of sentences in a book requires that the parts be understood in light of the whole.

Nothing in the higher, more complex processes themselves demand a new level of theory. Presumably some biological processes can be adequately accounted for simply in terms of chemistry, whereas others cannot. How do you decide? The coherence and explanatory power of the higher-level theory, not the phenomenon itself, suggest that biology is more than a subset of chemistry or religion more than a subset of psychology or sociology.

Some explanations do preclude others. Imagine that I see a shimmering light in my room at night and claim that I saw a ghost. If later investigation reveals that this shimmering light has been produced by a reflection from the streetlight by the mirror on my wall, I would be hard-pressed to continue maintaining that the light was really my long-deceased Aunt Mildred. The Newtonian model of the solar system as planets revolving around the sun precludes the ancient Mayan claim that the sun sets and rises because a great serpent swallows it each night and disgorges it each morning.

In contrast, enumerating the organic compounds that make up DNA and RNA tells us little about genetic processes without the addition of such nonmolecular constructs as "information transfer" or "cybernetic loop." A strictly chemical account does not preclude a biological one but, rather, both are required for a full understanding of genetic processes.

No new processes are at work in biology—all the elements, structures, and processes are those of physics and chemistry. More complex processes are still physical, chemical processes. Not new elements or forms but new theoretical concepts beyond those required by physics and chemistry are required to describe higher levels adequately. We don't need to invoke new physical entities; we do need to invoke new theoretical constructs. Nothing within a chemical analysis of life processes will demonstrate either the need for a new theoretical system or that a new level has emerged. This will become apparent only when a new theory is required to bring new coherence and explanation to the phenomena.

Likewise, psychoanalysis must insist that religion *as a human experience* is constituted by the same dynamics that constitute all human experiences. But a full account of religious experience may require more encompassing constructs, terms like *God, eternity,* or *life's purpose.* These terms take us beyond a list of psychodynamics just as an account of the theme of a book requires more than an enumeration of all the letters in the book, or just as an account of genetics requires more than isolated chemical formulas, or just as the study of Picasso's work requires more than a theory of pigmentation.

As opposed to the prior analysis, which focused on the discontinuity of disciplines, this model underscores the continuity between fields in a way that precludes the reduction of all disciplines to one. Chemistry builds on physics but also invokes new laws and theories; biology encompasses chemistry but also requires additional properties and concepts; the study of what Macmurray calls "the form of the personal" includes biology but also involves processes not wholly describable in biological terms, like intention (Kirkpatrick 1994a: chap. 5) and consciousness (Jones 1992b); theology requires the most encompassing and cosmic terms of all, like God, or Plotinus' One, or the Brahma of Hinduism, or the sunyata of Mahayana Buddhism. Physics is the most fundamental field and theology the most encompassing. The biological and human sciences are middle-level disciplines.

The Psychodynamics of Reductionism

Simply pointing out logical fallacies is surely not sufficient to disestablish the reductionist position in the psychoanalysis of religion. Like religious belief, metaphysical reductionism carries various unconscious dynamics, and its appeal is partly the appeal to those dynamics. I shall explore three possible unconscious roots of reductionism.

The Gendered Roots of Mechanism

One of the most radical aspects of Freud's project was the assumption that the very structures of knowledge reflect the dynamics of the psyche. All schools of psychology offer accounts of human motivation. Psychoanalysis goes on to insist that not only the drive to understand but also the forms of understanding reflect psychological forces. This must be as true of Freud's own reductionistic metaphysics as of the religious beliefs he opposed. Just as there is a psychoanalysis of belief, so there is also a psychoanalysis of unbelief.

One suggestion about the possible dynamics that power the reductionist philosophy come from those feminist psychoanalysts who have been among the most vigorous in pursuing the claim that knowledge, and especially Freud's beloved natural science, is itself dynamically conditioned and therefore gendered. The methods, categories, axioms, and commitments that shape our investigations of physical and social realities—including the reality of gender itself—are themselves gendered (Jones and Goldenberg 1992).

For Freud, maturity demands breaking free of attachment to the mother, renouncing infantile desires, and identifying with the power of the father. Such a move is possible only for the son; from this perspective the daughter's development is necessarily incomplete.

Central to the movement from Freudian to object relational paradigms has been the shift in focus from the oedipal to the pre-oedipal period. The father has been displaced by the primacy of the relationship with the mother. Seen from this perspective, male and not female development appears problematic. The girl growing up in relation to the mother remains connected to her primary object. The boy, however, breaks the identification with the mother (usually through aggression). Femininity represents empathic connection and caring; masculinity is defined by a defensive need for distance and a denial of connection (Chodorow 1989). When this masculine character-style becomes sublimated into the search for knowledge, the result looks like traditional

Western natural science, and its offshoots in the social sciences and empirical philosophy. Writes Chodorow, "This arelational masculinity, based on a need to dominate and deny women, the feminine, and human and natural interconnectedness, has become institutionalized in notions of scientific objectivity and technical rationality" (1989: 184).

It is not coincidental, then, that the modern age is characterized by Newtonian science, anomaic individualism, and an atomistic and uncaring vision of nature. A deeper analysis suggests that these factors—of which Freud's work is a monumental expression—reflect a one-sided reliance on the drive for separation and detachment, associated with masculinity. "A considerable literature has documented an extensive interpenetration between scientific, philosophical, and gender discourse. This literature has emerged in a critique of traditional notions of objectivity as deeply intertwined with traditional notions of masculinity" (Keller and Flax 1988: 337).

Beyond that, the ideal of objectivity central to the reductionist argument is predicated on a series of dichotomies. Both this dichotomous cognitive style and the content of the dichotomies themselves reflect the unconscious dynamics of gender. Write Keller and Flax,

> The same sexual division of emotional and intellectual labor that frames the maturation of male and female infants into adult men and women also, and simultaneously, divides the epistemological practices and bodies of knowledge we call science from those we call not-science. Modern science is constituted around a set of exclusionary oppositions in which what is named feminine is excluded and what is excluded—be it feeling, subjectivity, or nature—is named female. (Keller and Flax 1988: 337)

The myth of objectivity, in whose confines modern culture has conducted the search for knowledge, depends on dichotomous reasoning—objective versus subjective, outer versus inner, reason versus emotion—which itself reflects the "masculine" dynamic of separation.

The arguments of Chodorow and of Keller and Flax themselves depend on a radical dichotomizing of the genders and so do not necessarily move us beyond the dichotomizing style of thought that they (rightfully) regard as part of the problem. And by so tightly linking connection with femininity and separation with masculinity, such a theory has trouble accounting for the relational theories written by men. Freud and much of nineteenth- and early twentieth-century science (and theology) were phallic and aggressive and masculine. But equally masculine are the relational theologies of Schleiermacher and Buber and the relational psychoanalysis of Winnicott, Fairbairn, and Guntrip. A similar point about Chodorow and Keller in relation to philosophy is made by Moi (1989). My own critique of Chodorow et al., following Moi, can be found in Jones (in press a), in which I question how detachment and caregiving become dichotomized and gendered in their argument, and question their reduction of the feminine to the maternal and the rejection of any role for "the law of the father" other than to be oppressive.

The infant research as reviewed by Stern, Lichtenberg, and others does not seem to find a distinction between the genders. Infant boys and girls begin life as selves-in-relation and continue to develop in a single pattern of development. Women do not remain more relational while men become more independent. Culture pushes boys to accentuate independence and girls to be more passive, but what Chodorow and Keller see as essential developmental patterns are, rather, the result of patriarchal culture. The aggressively reductive sciences of modernity may well be the expression of masculine development, but only masculine development as shaped by patriarchal society. (A parallel point about the dichotomizing of narcissism and object love is made by Layton [1990].)

A way past this dichotomy of masculine objectivity versus femininity is implied by Winnicott in his discussion of object use and object relating. There he suggests that objectivity is created by an act of aggression (Keller 1985: 91n6; Jones in press b). By attempting and failing to destroy the object, the child learns of its independent existence (Winnicott 1971: 93). Winnicott points to the conjunction of objectification and aggression whereby objectification is an act of fruitful aggression against the object. Certainly people report that being treated in a totally objective way ("like just a number") often feels like an act of aggression against them. Thus a certain amount of aggression may be endemic to the scientific enterprise, with its phallic language of "tackling problems" and "penetrating solutions." As Keller (1985, 1992) points out, such aggression is often directed at nature (and other human beings) in the form of domination. Perhaps the undermining of the myth of absolute objectivity in contemporary philosophy of science and its replacement by a less traditionally masculine and more mutual metaphor of interaction and interconnection, if introjected into the psyches of scientists and therefore into the deep structure of science itself, might result in a less aggressive and dominance-oriented science.

A gender-sensitive psychoanalysis reveals how reductionistic science expresses the desires of the unconscious, not only in terms of motivation but also in its content and practice, and also reveals that these desires may reflect the different developmental trajectories of boys and girls. Specifically Freud and much of modernity idealized that combination of investigation by detached observation, a motivation to dominate and control nature, and an impersonal model of the universe, all of which serve as sublimations of the need for distance and separation. Men (and women) find such reductionistic methods and images compelling to the extent that their character is fashioned around the same unconscious drive for distance.

THE DISOWNING OF SUBJECTIVE EXPERIENCE

I often encounter a form of self-experience that, paradoxically, seeks to deny the reality of self-experience. This phenomenon has a cultural context. The obsession of the modern age becomes control. And technology has given us the means to act out that obsession. We assume that we must control everything: the weather, the course of the economy, the production of children. Clinically, one of the major symptoms of our age seems to be the fear of losing control. Many an ulcer, hypertensive state, and anxiety attack begins when the men and women of modernity sense their lives, or parts of them, slipping out of their control. Time and time again a major root of sexual dysfunction, hesitancy about intimacy, or conflicts around the having and raising of children turns out to be the fear of losing control.

Our obsessive drive for control often invades family life as well. The sanctuary of child rearing cannot remain forever protected from the attitudes that are beaten into us by the media, leap out of our textbooks, govern our commence, and shape our view of the world. Frequently I see families whose fundamental concern in coming to a therapist is not improving communication or knowing their children better but only finding ways of ensuring that the kids will turn out all right, like the latest product off the assembly line.

Psychologically there appears to be a connection between the cultural values of control and detachment and a fear of subjective experience, especially emotional experience. Existing outside the perimeters of reason and often threatening to break down our carefully wrought walls of control, affect appears dangerous, chaotic, or threatening. Often its existence is simply denied.

I have patients who seem oblivious to whole realms of life. Of course, I am a good parent (or husband, or wife), they say. I provide a nice house, new toys, stimulating vacations, good education, and, sometimes, expensive therapists. These are not (usually) bad or malevolent people; they speak in all sincerity and perplexity, occasionally laced with an anger bred of incomprehension. Vainly do their children (or spouses) try to convey to them their appreciation for that bounty and their sense that something crucial is still missing.

Bollas (1987) writes about what he calls the "normotic personality." Although this is not exactly the same phenomenon I wish to describe, there are certain resonances. The normotic personality rejects any intrusions of subjectivity and seeks to become entirely objective, to see himself or herself as an object in a world of objects. The normotic personality collects facts and "takes refuge in material objects" (Bollas 1987: 138). Normotics may seem more bonded to machines than to people. They may describe themselves in quasi-mechanical terms, in a discourse purged of subjectivity. I often say to such patients that they are describing their life story as though it happened to someone else: all the external details and no account of what it was actually like. This is more than just a blunting of appropriate affect; such persons seem completely disconnected from their own lives.

This refusal of subjectivity in the name of total objectification is readily expressed by a reductionistic science that seeks to collapse the kaleidoscope of human experience into a mechanical system. Here again modern culture reinforces the refusal of subjectivity by propounding theories that reduce subjective experience to mechanical activity and by broadcasting models of the mind as a computer or electrochemical machine. I am not arguing against the usefulness of such metaphors (although from a logical standpoint I find them uncompelling; see Jones 1992b for some of the reasons why) but, rather, asking what psychodynamic forces drive such models and make them attractive. A reductionistic theory which says that consciousness is unreal correlates comfortably with that form of self-experience which, paradoxically, seeks to deny self-experience.

Bollas (1987) remarks on the recurrent theme in contemporary literature and media of the person who turns out to be a robot. This theme is not a prophecy of future technology, Bollas suggests, but a metaphor for a contemporary personality type. And, I might add, it is a metaphor for contemporary reductionistic models of the self, which often portray human beings as computers or other machines.

THE REFUSAL TO ENTER THE TRANSITIONAL SPACE

We have seen how Freud's single-minded allegiance to the reality principle dichotomized the world into camps—truth and falsity, reality and delusion—and how Winnicott moved beyond this dichotomy by proposing a "third area of human living, one neither inside the individual nor outside" (1971: 110). Transitional experience transcends the dichotomy of objectivity and subjectivity, for it is an "intermediate area of *experiencing*" (1971: 2). From a reductionistic epistemological perspective, the transitional process appears paradoxical, for it is neither subjective or objective but contains elements of both (Jones 1992a). Such an experience requires the capacity for disciplined imagination, which Paul Tillich calls "ecstatic reason." These experiences are, in William James's terminology, "noetic"—that is, they are a source of knowledge. But they are also interior and ecstatic. That is, this kind of experience does not fit within the categories of a dichotomizing reductionism, which cannot count beyond two.

In their research using projective cards detailing pictures of people engaging in various devotional practices in order to investigate religious experience, the Saurs describe one category of response as the refusal to enter the transitional space (Saur and Saur 1993, n.d.). And Bollas (1987) writes often of patients who have lost the capacity to play. Reductionistic metaphysics can serve to express and rationalize this one-dimensional approach to living.

A reductionistic methodology is hardly psychologically neutral. Like all epistemological claims, it too expresses certain unconscious dynamics. It carries the stereotypical masculine drive for objectivity and control. It facilitates the refusal of subjective experience in the name of a totalizing objectivity. It rationalizes the loss of the capacity for transitional experience. These dynamics give a reductionistic methodology an appeal despite its overriding logical difficulties.

7

A Nonreductive Psychoanalysis

Although reductionism played a salient role in the development of psychoanalysis, it is methodologically suspect. What might take the place of reductionism, especially in the psychoanalysis of religion?

Nonreductive Approaches to Religious Symbols

Freud's analysis, Hans Loewald says, "always smacks of reduction. It also implies there is some element of sham or pretense in our greatly valued higher activities" (1978: 75). By contrast, for Loewald, mental activity is not primarily a defense but, rather, "belongs to the area of ego development" (1988: 33) and represents a real transformation of instinct. Sublimation gives rise to genuinely new forms of thought, which still remain in touch with their source in the unconscious. These higher mental processes—what Freud called "secondary process"—arise out of our instinctual nature, but our "primary processes" must always remain accessible. As the source of reason, the unconscious has a rationality all its own in which dichotomies are transcended and a unity apprehended. Immersion in this primary process points to important ways of knowing that are "structured or centered differently" from linear reason (1978: 68). By advocating a "more comprehensive perspective" on human knowledge, Loewald represents a far richer vision of human experience than Freud's—a vision in which there is a "new level of consciousness, of conscire, on which primary and secondary modes of mentation may be known together" (Loewald 1978: 65).

In a careful exegesis of Freud's *Civilization and Its Discontents,* Loewald (1978) shows how religion and art serve to keep us open to ways of knowing and being that are rooted in the primary process, with its unitary and timeless sensibility.

> If we are willing to admit that instinctual life and religious life both betoken forms of experience that underlie and go beyond conscious and personalized forms of mentation—beyond those forms of mental life, of ordering our world, on which we stake so much—then we may be at a point where psychoanalysis can begin to contribute in its own way to the understanding of religious experience, instead of ignoring or rejecting its genuine validity or treating it as a mark of human immaturity. (1978: 73)

Religion and art are not simply raw expressions of the unconscious. But, unlike more abstract forms of conscious rationality, in religion and art the "experience of unity [with the primary process] is restored, or at least evoked, in the form of symbolic linkage" (1988: 45). Symbols evoke the experience of the primary process in such a way that all differentiation is not lost. They draw us into a psychic realm in which we experience our connection with the primary process—experiences characterized by timelessness and unity—but in such a way that we do not lose our capacity for secondary process, unlike the schizophrenic, who is so engulfed in the unconscious that all conscious rationality ceases (1988: 52–65). Symbols are not purely the product either of the unconscious (like a dream) or of linear rationality but are influenced by both levels of the mind.

Religious symbols are a primary vehicle of this "return, on a higher level of organization, to the early magic of thought, gesture, word, image, emotion, fantasy, as they become united again with what in ordinary nonmagical experience they only reflect, recollect, represent or symbolize . . . a mourning of lost original oneness and a celebration of oneness regained." (1988: 81). By reformulating the primary process in more positive terms and defending the "general validity or importance in human life of the different spheres and forms of experience" (1978: 71), Loewald appreciates imaginative and symbolic processes in ways that Freud—with his negative view of the primary process—never could.

Our earliest mental state is not simply to be renounced or outgrown (as Freud thought) but, rather, to be returned to time and time again. Such returns are sources of creativity and refreshment.

According to Winnicott, the child's experience with transitional objects is neither objective or subjective. Instead transitional experience can be called interactional, for it begins to form in the interactional space between the mother and the infant. Transitional experience takes place in a "potential space . . . its foundation is the baby's trust in the mother *experienced* over a long-enough period" (1971: 110). Good-enough caretaking provides the infant with enough trust in life's dependability that development is not thwarted and the infant can venture beyond the perimeter of his or her private world. The transitional process from which symbols arise is clearly an interpersonal experience—first in relation to the mother and later in relation to the "whole cultural field" (1971: 100).

Play closes the gap between subjectivity and objectivity that Cartesian empiricism had opened. "In playing, the child manipulates external phenomena in the service of the dream and invests chosen external phenomena with dream meaning and feeling" (1971: 51). The infusion of meaning from the inner world into actions and objects in the public sphere, or the expression of inner-generated truths by means of external physical and verbal forms, describes not only children playing with teddy bears and empty boxes but also the creation of symphonies, sculptures, novels, and even scientific theories. Winnicott's theory is not primarily about stuffed animals and blankets but is, rather, about how certain kinds of interpersonal experiences give rise to the process of symbolization. For "cultural experience [is] an extension of the idea of transitional phenomena and of play" (1971: 99).

Having moved from the world of pure subjectivity into a less responsive external world, the self is forever caught in the tension of inner and outer and the struggle to relate its personal longings and insights to the unresponsive "not-me world" of objects (1971: 1). Thus the desire to integrate or transcend the dichotomy of inner and outer, subjective and objective, lives on long after the teddy bear has been forgotten. When transitional objects are outgrown, they leave behind the creativity that drives the arts and the curiosity that drives the sciences, that is, the capacity to create culture. In an oft-quoted and moving passage about the fate of transitional objects, Winnicott writes,

> Its fate is to be gradually allowed to be decathected, so that in the course of years it becomes not so much forgotten as relegated to limbo. By this I mean that in health the transitional object does not "go inside" nor does the feeling about it necessarily undergo repression. It is not forgotten and it is not mourned. It loses meaning, and this is because the transitional phenomena have become diffused, have become spread out over the whole intermediate territory between "inner psychic reality" and "the external world as perceived by two persons in common," that is to say, over the whole cultural field. At this point my subject widens out into that of play, and of artistic creativity and appreciation, and of religious feeling, and of dreaming. (1971: 5)

In discussing transitional objects, Winnicott is not talking about just "child's play" but is proposing nothing less than a psychoanalytic theory of culture that begins from the interpersonal matrix of infant and parent, moves to the development of creativity through play and the use of transitional objects, and ends with the symphonies of Ludwig van Beethoven, the paintings of Rembrandt van Rijn, and the theories of Einstein. "For cultural experience, including its most sophisticated developments, the position is the *potential space* between the baby and the mother" (1971: 107). Culture, science, religion, and art are thus normal extensions of the transitional realm. For Freud the laws, institutions, and creative activities of culture are defenses against fratricide, foreign structures heteronomously imposed on the individual in the service of instinctual control (Flax 1990: 119). For Winnicott cultural creations and institutions develop naturally from the pleasures of the intermediate world.

Summarizing his disparate thoughts on this subject, Winnicott writes,

> I have tried to draw attention to the importance both in theory

and in practice of a third area, that of play, which expands into creative living and into the whole cultural life of man. This third area has been contrasted with inner or personal psychic reality and with the actual world in which the individual lives, which can be objectively perceived. I have located this important area of *experience* in the potential space between the individual and the environment. . . . it is here that the individual experiences creative living. (1971: 102–103)

In contrast to Freud, Winnicott proposes an independent line of development for the symbolic process that starts from the play of children and leads to the theories of high-energy physics, the complex melodies of Mozart, the evocative symbols of the world's major faiths. Winnicott suggests that the symbolic order (which is really all of culture) cannot be reduced to the vicissitudes of drives but, rather, has its own line of development. The symbolic process is not derived from instinctual dissatisfaction nor does it exist only to serve biological needs. Rather, the symbolic process arises naturally out of spontaneous true-self creativity, first on the part of the child and later on the part of the adult as well. The transitional sphere derives from the impulse of the true self toward creativity and self-expression. Winnicott presents here a strong argument for the integrity of the symbolic world, which appeals to those for whom the symbols of religion or art play an important role.

Beyond these concerns—which bear directly on the epistemological status of psychoanalysis and religion, as well as those of art and natural science—another aspect of the transitional process is relevant to religion. For Winnicott and Loewald, human life is impoverished if deprived of access to the transitional realm, or to what Loewald (1978) calls the "primary level of mentation." Reimmersion in the primary process through moments of rapture and ecstasy are necessary times of psychic refreshment and rejuvenation and are the source of creativity, sanity, and a full human life. Winnicott's transitional process means not only a developmental stage or the use of certain soon-to-be-outgrown objects but also a certain transitional state of consciousness or psychological space. Teddy bears and blankets are hopefully put aside, but the capacity to enter and

re-enter that transitional consciousness where the subject-object dualism of "objectifying mentation" (Loewald 1978: 51) is transcended abides
as the source of "creative living" (Winnicott 1971: 100) and a deeper rationality.

The significance of Winnicott and Loewald for religion lies in their
advocacy of this richness of consciousness and of entering again and
again into that transforming psychological space from which renewal
and creativity emerge. The rituals, words, and introspective methods of
religion have traditionally been a major source of the disciplined imagination and of the evocation of those epistemically creative and psychologically restorative transitional experiences.

In different terms Winnicott and Loewald both propose an independent developmental line for symbolic processes and emphasize the importance for mental health of experiences that go beyond the dichotomy
of subjectivity and objectivity. This may explain part of their appeal to
psychoanalysts concerned with religious and spiritual issues, for they
each provide nonreductive psychoanalytic frameworks in which the
analysis of religion can take place.

William Meissner and Ana-Maria Rizzuto

Meissner and Rizzuto build on Winnicott's work to develop psychoanalytically informed understandings of religious symbolism. Meissner
(1984) emphasizes the location of transitional phenomena on the border
between objectivity and subjectivity. Religious symbols, neither subjective nor objective, belong neither to the objective domain of physical
things nor to the subjective world of hallucination and daydream.

The crucifix, the Star of David, ritual gestures and vestments, sacred
texts and phrases, and holy shrines all involve objects in the world of
space and time but they are, for the believer, not only physical and temporal. They are "not to be envisioned merely in terms of their physical
attributes. The crucifix is not just a piece of carved wood, nor the Torah
simply a roll of parchment with ancient writing on it" (Meissner 1984:
181). To describe the botanical species of tree from which a crucifix is
carved or the chemical composition of the ink used to inscribe the Torah

is to miss the believer's point. The cross is made from wood and the Torah from ink, but in a religious context they become vehicles for meanings that go beyond botany and calligraphy.

For Meissner such symbolization is transitional because the "objects as religious symbols are neither exclusively perceived in real and objective terms, nor simply produced by subjective creation. Rather, they evolve from the amalgamation of what is real, material, and objective as it is experienced, penetrated, and creatively reshaped by the subjective belief and patterns of meaning attributed to the object by the believer" (1984: 181). Such symbols stand at the interface of subjective and objective worlds, using physical, artistic, and linguistic objects to convey a spiritual or moral meaning.

Beyond that, "such symbols become part of the transitional realm of the believer's illusory experience" (Meissner 1984: 181), that is, they are used in the context of a certain psychological space or state of consciousness. Transitional phenomena are bearers of a special kind of experience. They involve not only specific objects—blankets, teddy bears, fingers—but, more important, a specific psychological space or state of consciousness.

In her research into the origin and transformations of the individual's "god representation," Ana-Maria Rizzuto (1979) explicitly locates the reality of God in the "transitional space," halfway between sheer hallucination and physical reality. In this realm of imagination, the child creates a private but real world of transitional objects—imaginary friends, security blankets, personal games, and magical beliefs. Rizzuto is quite consciously attempting to validate the importance of fantasy and the imagination for mental health, as opposed to Freud's empirical austerity (see Rizzuto 1979: 46–53). God is, for Rizzuto, a creation of the imagination, but that is, for her, precisely the source of God's power and reality, for we cannot live without the creations of our imagination.

> We have forgotten the powerful reality of nonexistent objects, objects of our creation. . . . The fictive creations of our minds . . . have as much regulatory potential in our psychic function as people around us in the flesh. . . . Human life is impoverished when

these immaterial characters made out of innumerable experiences
vanish under the repression of a psychic realism that does violence
to the ceaseless creativity of the human mind. In this sense, at least,
religion is not an illusion. It is an integral part of being human,
truly human in our capacity to create nonvisible but meaningful
realities. . . . Without those fictive realities human life becomes a
dull animal existence. (1979: 47)

Religious symbols thus gain their power as carriers of the realm of the
imagination.

Meissner and Rizzuto find in Winnicott's work a psychological location for religious phenomena. They find in Winnicott a nonreductive
understanding of the function of religious symbols: such symbols mark
out an intellectual territory intermediate between objectivity and subjectivity and facilitate the use of imagination. The importance of transitional objects lies in their capacity to evoke a necessary but paradoxical
experience that takes us beyond objectivity and subjectivity.

Paul Pruyser

A precursor to Rizzuto's and Meissner's use of Winnicott in the psychology of religion can be found in the writings of Paul Pruyser. Like Winnicott, Pruyser senses that the modern dichotomy of factuality and delusion is too rigid. Too much of reality is left unaccounted for. "Primary
process and secondary process, autism and pure objectivity, are not exclusive options. There is a third, transcendent sphere, a special level of
thought and action which combines strands of premises and meanings
into a kind of experience that has its own validity, *its own consensual val-
idation.* A story becomes a myth only when it is widely accepted and
given the status of ultimate wisdom or sacred knowledge" (Pruyser 1974:
217). This "illusionistic sphere is a kind of third world that lies between
above the other two worlds with which human beings have to contend"
(Malony and Spilka 1991: 165). Like Winnicott, Pruyser uses Freud's
term, *illusion,* for this alternative reality, but he wants to redeem the term
from the negative connotations Freud gave it. "Illusion is neither hallu-

cination or delusion . . . nor is it straightforward sense perception" (Malony and Spilka 1991: 166).

The "illusionistic world" stands midway (literally, on the chart that Pruyser draws to illustrate his point) between the "autistic world" of pure, unconstrained fantasy and the "realistic world" of "hard, undeniable facts" (Malony and Spilka 1991: 177). This illusionistic world is characterized by "tutored fantasy, adventurous thinking, orderly imagination, inspired connections, imaginative entities or events, symbols, playing, [and the] transcendent object prefigured by the child's transitional object" (Malony and Spilka 1991: 177).

Pruyser is concerned about the ways the imaginative world is threatened either by psychopathology, which pulls the imagination in the direction of narcissistic projections and hallucinations, or by a heavy-handed realism that "works to curtail the novelty-producing, potentially creative imagination nurtured in the illusionistic sphere" (Malony and Spilka 1991: 184). Pruyser wants to protect the illusionistic sphere from these threats because, like Winnicott, he sees this realm as necessary for creativity and he knows that life becomes impoverished and one-dimensional without the products of the imagination.

For Pruyser the psychological roots of religion lie in the illusionistic sphere. From the play of the imagination comes forth the beliefs, rituals, and stories that become the core of a religion. More specifically, Pruyser suggests that the image of a transcendental reality grows from the child's experience with transitional objects. Pruyser directly asserts that the "transitional object is the transcendent" (Malony and Spilka 1991: 163) in that it exists "beyond the ordinary division we make between the mental image produced by the mind itself and the objective perceptual image produced by the real word impinging upon the sensory system" (Malony and Spilka 1991: 163). But he does not lay out in any detail the stages of development by which the blanket and the teddy bear are transformed into the idea of God.

While beginning from the desire to go beyond the dichotomy of fact and fantasy, Pruyser's solution is simply to slip a third area in between these two. They remain the same opposing domains as in Freud's positivistic science. The third area is introduced in a way that does not affect or transform our conceptions of either narcissism or "hard, undeniable facts." Pruyser realizes that the "determination to flee from all illusions in the name of radical rationality . . . is an illusion in its own right" (1974: 204) and that "illusionistic thinking pertains to . . . the spirit of science" (Malony and Spilka 1991: 177). But the "realistic world" remains one of "look-and-see referents [and] actual entities and events" (Malony and Spilka 1991: 177). Unfortunately the dichotomy between subjectivity and objectivity, fantasy and factuality, cannot be overcome by simply adding a third category. A more radical restructuring of our understanding of human knowledge is called for, one that does not leave the old positivistic image of the realistic world intact but, rather, transforms our thinking about our thinking about the physical world. Rather than segregating religious (and artistic) knowing into a third type of knowledge, I argue for a more radical epistemological transformation that underscores the imaginative and illusionistic nature of *all* forms of human understanding.

The Ontology of the Transitional Sphere

The currently popular Winnicottian approach to religion, represented by Meissner, Rizzuto, and Pruyser, assimilates religious phenomena to transitional objects and raises the question of the ontological status of objects in the transitional realm. The term *transitional* has two rather different referents: (1) those objects, like blankets and teddy bears, that are, as Winnicott says, "neither inside nor outside," and (2) a state of consciousness or mode of experience, a "transitional space," which transcends the dualism of inner and outer, subjective and objective. Elsewhere I have suggested that in their use of Winnicott, Meissner and Rizzuto focus more on the first referent and much less on the second (Jones 1991a). I want to argue that the second meaning, the transitional mode of *experiencing*, is the most important one for the psychological understanding of religion.

For Meissner, religious faith, God representations, symbols, and prayer all stand on the border between objectivity and subjectivity. Religion "represents a realm in which the subjective and the objective interpenetrate" (Meissner 1984: 178). The believer brings his or her personal experience to the process of believing, but faith is not purely subjective. Its contents are grounded in the traditions and experiences of others in an organized community and relate to the nature of the world, of human existence, of value, and of the presence of the spiritual realm. Thus, "both the subjective and objective poles of experience contribute to the substance of belief" (Meissner 1984: 178).

The God representation, Meissner writes, is neither purely subjective, like a hallucination, nor "is it totally beyond the reach of subjectivity; rather it is located, in Winnicott's terms, 'outside, inside, at the border'" (Meissner 1984: 179). The individual's God representation emerges from the tension between his or her own private experience (Rizzuto 1979) and the images and metaphors for God provided by the individual's culture. It belongs neither to the individual's private world nor to the surrounding religious environment but is, rather, a synthesis of the two.

Meissner labels as transitional the use of physical, artistic, and linguistic objects to convey a spiritual or moral meaning because the "objects as religious symbols are neither exclusively perceived in real and objective terms, nor simply produced by subjective creation" (Meissner 1984: 181). In all these areas Meissner does not emphasize the capacity for play, symbolization, creativity, and other activities carried on in what Winnicott calls the transitional space. Meissner lessens Winnicott's focus on the interpersonal world and emphasizes instead the interplay of subjective and objective factors in the constellation of transitional objects. This focus yields, for Meissner, a viable location for religious symbols that, for him, belongs neither to the totally objective domain of physical objects in the world of space and time nor to the purely subjective world of hallucination and daydream.

When writing about transitional objects, however, Winnicott was calling attention to a certain capacity for *experience*. While security blankets are left behind, this capacity to transcend the dichotomies of inner and outer, subjective and objective, continues to grow and becomes the basis for human creativity in the arts, sciences, and throughout culture, becoming "diffused . . . spread out over the whole cultural field" (Winnicott 1979: 14). Imagination represents more than a world of ghosts and fairy tales; it is the source of the plays of Shakespeare and the formulas of Einstein. Watching a child play with a teddy bear, Winnicott saw a child developing the capacity to write a novel or invent a machine or propose a theory.

Rizzuto (1979) also explicitly locates the reality of God in the transitional space. In doing so, Rizzuto insists on the importance of fantasy and the imagination for mental health. In writing about the reality of transitional objects, Rizzuto clearly uses *real* to mean "powerful." Such "fictive" entities as "muses, guardian angels, heroes . . . the Devil, God himself . . . unseen atoms, imaginary chemical formulas" (1979: 27) can have a powerful impact on human lives, and their psychic power constitutes their reality. Imaginary playmates and abstract ideas perform an indispensable psychological function in the lives of individuals and cultures, and so the imaginative capacity demands respect rather than denigration.

While trading heavily on the term *imagination,* Rizzuto struggles to avoid the ontological question of the reality of these transitional or imaginary creations. Winnicott, as usual, treats this question in a few vague but tantalizing sentences. Transitional objects, Winnicott suggests, are both created and found: "In health the infant creates what is in fact lying around waiting to be found. But in health *the object is created, not found.* . . . A good object is no good to the infant unless created by the infant. . . . Yet the object must be found in order to be created. This has to be accepted as a paradox, and not solved by a restatement that, by its cleverness, seems to eliminate the paradox" (Winnicott 1965: 181).

It is this paradox that Rizzuto refers to in her discussion of the reality status of transitional objects. "In ordinary language . . . illusory and real are antithetical, mutually exclusive concepts. This is not so in the private realm of transitional reality where illusory and real dimensions of experience interpenetrate each other to such an extent that they cannot be teased apart without destroying what is essential in the experience" (Rizzuto 1979: 27). For Winnicott, the transitional space transcends the dichotomy of subjectivity and objectivity. This is a claim about the state of consciousness labeled transitional. Meissner and Rizzuto suggest that it also is a claim about the various *objects* labeled as transitional, including

God, who "is a psychically created object who is also 'found'" (Rizzuto 1979: 87). Thus, with the help of Winnicott's terminology, Meissner and Rizzuto try to chart an intermediate course between psychological reductionism (God as created) and a kind of theological objectivism (God as found).

Rizzuto's advocacy of imagination and Meissner's refurbishing of illusion speak more to the process of knowing than to the reality of what is known. It is not clear exactly what ontological status is attributed to a God who intermingles subjective and objective features (as in Meissner) or who is both created and found (as in Rizzuto). But what does it mean to ask about the ontological status of transitional phenomena? Does the question tacitly presuppose that there are only two real realms of existence: the subjective reality of self-awareness and the objective reality of things existing apart from ourselves? (For some reductionists the subjective reality does not really exist either.) Our previous analysis collapsed this dichotomy. Even objective things like tables and chairs, to say nothing of electrons, black holes, and genes, are both created and found: Created by the metaphors and categories through which and in which we find them. They may well have some existence apart from us, but they exist in our knowledge as tables, chairs, electrons, black holes, and genes by virtue of the schemata through which we encounter them.

So powerful is the grip of the Cartesian dichotomy of subjectivity and objectivity that we cannot seem to find a way out of it except by using its terms and speaking of things as both created *and* found, inner *and* outer, and by calling them transitional objects between these two domains. Clearly certain experiences are amalgamations of so-called objective and subjective factors. Perhaps "in health" (as Winnicott says) virtually all experience is like that (such is certainly the claim of the philosophers of science discussed previously). But if we ask whether the transitional realm is *really* there, we probably mean "there independent of us." And, of course, by definition the transitional realm is not independent of us. But nor is it totally our own creation. Nor is there any realm of reality *that we know* which is completely independent of us, as the very act of knowing it (and knowing its independence of us) implies our interaction with it. Our knowledge that the world is independent of us is not itself independent of us but comes only through our interaction with and categorization of the world of our experience.

So is there a transitional realm that really exists (that is, which is not a hallucination or daydream) but that does not exist independently of us? Of course! That describes the world of tables, chairs, electrons, black holes, and genes as well as of symphonic music and poetry. These things we only know "from interaction" (Lakoff and Johnson 1980) with them. These things, like all things, we know only as we stand in relation to them.

Freud's theory of development from narcissism to object appreciation was an epistemology as well as a theory of human nature. And it was an epistemology consistent with what Freud knew of human nature as a system of objective forces and mechanisms. Likewise, a relational paradigm is both an epistemology and a theory of human nature. Here our nature is to be in relation; we live and die (and also know and understand) in relation. Such a relational epistemology is consistent with a relational view of human nature.

Where does religion fit into this? Macmurray, Buber and others have argued that the eternal you is known only by standing in relation to her. Buber thought that was unique to God. A relational epistemology suggests that is true of all knowing. As Arbib and Hesse said, we do not suddenly wear a different hat with regard to "truth" when speaking of God from that which we wear for doing natural science (1986:161). All knowing is relational knowing, and all the claims we make arise out of being in relation. The objects of religious knowledge, like all objects, exist in an interactional space.

The epistemically important question, then, is, how do we enter into a relationship with the natural world so that we can know its atomic constitution, or how do we enter into a relationship with God so we can experience the divine presence? The answer is, through specific disciplines. Through the study of physics I interact with the world in such a way as to come to know the world as a system of physical laws and forces. Through such spiritual disciplines as prayer, devotion, meditation, and ritual I train my consciousness to experience the divine (the epistemological importance of such disciplines is developed in Jones 1981, 1995).

Moshe Halevi Spero

A rather different response to the problem of reductionism is articulated by Moshe Halevi Spero. His argument has both clinical and epistemological components. Clinically Spero insists that not accepting a religious patient's view that God is objectively real may constitute a profound failure of empathy, which can shipwreck the therapy. It is not sufficient that the therapist listen respectfully and interpret nonreductively. For Spero, establishing a working alliance with a religious patient requires empathizing with the patient's conviction that God exists (Spero 1990; see also McDargh 1993).

Making such a stance psychologically coherent requires that Spero articulate a framework in which God's existence makes sense. This he attempts in *Religious Objects as Psychological Structures* (1992), where he seeks to "link the therapeutic process directly to an underlying religious structure with built-in potential for relationship with God" (1992: 97). Spero insists that "if God exists, then from both the psychological as well as religious point of view, God *is* an object! Something about this being and its relationship with humankind must be representable, even if ephemerally and precariously. . . . some initial meeting point between the human mind and a perceptually veridical object must remain implicit throughout. It does not even matter if the individual can ever consciously recollect perceiving this primordial object as an objectively external one" (1992: 89). In other words, not only does God exist "out there" but God "holding forth the possibility of being discovered or known may be further assumed to have created mechanisms or faculties through which discovery is indeed possible" (1992: 140).

According to Spero, God has implanted in the human psyche certain "deocentric intrapsychic endowments," which serve as precursors of the experience of God (1992: 139). Made directly by God, such structures are a priori, existing before psychological experiencing. Created in the image of God, the infant has some primordial, preverbal awareness of God's presence. Spero quotes Roy Shafer to the effect that "it is conceivable that some objects have existed as internal objects from their beginnings" (Spero likes this sentence so much he quotes it twice: Spero 1992: 89, 191).

Such primordial awareness may constitute "deep preconceptions on the order of an 'archaic heritage' that disposes the psyche towards God's presence" (1992: 142).

The individual's personal God representation is not, however, a direct consequence of this primordial awareness of the deity. The God representation is internally generated, an "amalgamation of suitable material, some of which is supplied by family and social input, which is then projected and given quasi-objective form" (1992: 138). Spero is therefore arguing for two lines of religious development. One involves the internalization of our experience of objects in our ordinary world and the constellation of a *private* God representation in much the same way as described by Rizzuto, McDargh, and others. The second, and this is the core of Spero's position, involves "an *objective* God object moving on *its* representational pathway toward internalization" (1992: 138).

Such a deocentric process of internalization is possible because there is both an objectively real God and a literally God-given compatibility between the developmental structures of the human psyche and that objective God they are designed to grasp. Although the term "internalized God representation" is widely used in the literature (by Rizzuto, McDargh, Meissner, and others) to cover variations on the first, intrapsychic processes, Spero insists that only the second, deocentric process can truly be said to yield an internalized God representation. "While the line of development for the objective, *human* object may, indeed, yield anthropocentrically based, internal or endopsychic gods, only the line of development from the objective object known as God can legitimately be said to yield an *internalized* God representation. For only in the later case has something *really* external and objectively of God been taken inward" (1992: 138). This then raises the obvious question, "To whom do we relate, to God or to the representation of God?" (1992: 142). The answer is equally obvious: to both. That is, we relate to God through our representation of God just as we relate to our parents through our internalized representation of them.

Thus Spero wants to preserve both what he takes to be the religiously essential claim that God is objectively real and the clinically essential claim that our representation of God can be distorted by the vicissitudes of our development. He preserves them by articulating two separate lines of development: an intrapsychic one and a deocentric one. These lines interact, and at any given moment an individual's religious experience is a conjunction of his or her internalized experience of the real God and his or her private, intrapsychically generated God representation. Thus Spero does not naively identify our experience or representations of God with God. Such a literal identification would involve us in idolatry and, at a psychological level, in violating the prohibition against images and would render clinical analysis of an individual's religious experience sacrilegious. Thus Spero gives the clinician free reign to analyze and interpret the individual's religious expressions and beliefs while also preserving God's objective reality by locating our connection to the real God in a separate, semi-autonomous developmental realm.

Spero wants to make room within psychoanalysis for the existence of God by making God into another external object that we internalize and project back onto our intrapsychic representations in a way precisely analogous to our relationships with parents and other primary objects. So, in answering the question whether we relate to an objective God or to our God representation, Spero quotes Sandler's discussion of our relationship to our mother, in which he says, "The internal image of the mother is thus not a substitute for an object relationship, but is itself an indispensable part of the relationship" (1992: 142). The same, for Spero, can be said of our relationship to God.

Sorenson (1993) rightly calls Spero's epistemology pre-Kantian. That is, Spero wants psychology to disregard the disciplinary limits I articulated earlier and to discuss God and not just the human experience of God. Spero rejects Kant's insistence on the limitations of the human mind and also rejects the limitations of finite human psychological structures to grasp the infinite. Rather, Spero believes that God fashioned the human mind in order to know God, and so our faculties are designed to correlate with the divine reality. Paraphrasing Moses Maimonides in contemporary psychological language, Spero writes: "Just as He addresses man through psychological structures within which He has planted His image, seeing as man is, after all, a psychological, object-seeking being; so, too, shall you address Him through psychological

structures, seeing as He wishes to make Himself available as object"
(1992: 30).

Within the context of particular religious faith, which begins from
the premise of God's existence, such a position makes sense, although
every religious person is not required to accept Spero's epistemology.
Spero asserts that "we have no idea what God, indeed, *is* like" (1992: 29),
so it is not clear what sort of knowing of God comes to us through our
primordial experience and divinely created categories. From a perspective encompassing world religions, the pluralism of experiences and ar-
ticulations may be too broad to fit within this framework. Spero acknowledges that "God is apparently known in different ways by different
people during different eras" (1990: 69), but it is not clear that the same
set of cognitive and psychological structures can be correlated with, say,
the divine lawgiver of Mount Sinai and the universal sunyata (emptiness)
of Mahayana Buddhism. Or is the sacred encountered through a different set of psychological processes in the different religious traditions?

As long as Spero stays strictly within the Orthodox Jewish context out
of which he is writing, the particularities of his exposition are no problem.
If, however, the student of religion wants to use Spero's model to make
sense of the plurality of world religions from a nonreductive, psychoanalytic standpoint, some broadening of the categories will be necessary.
More specifically, the primordial awareness might be understood as a
generic drive for something sacred and transcendent to serve as the ground
of value and the source of meaning and purpose to life. Such a primordial
drive may be structured and expressed differently as it is refashioned by
the interpersonal experiences, cognitive categories, and cultural formula-
tions that mediate the experience of the sacred to each individual.

Such a primordial awareness bears some relationship to what Christo-
pher Bollas (1987) calls the "unthought known." These are the bodily sensations, primitive smells and sights associated with objects, and the experience of interacting with them, that the child incorporates before the
dawning of mental representation and language. "All children store the
quality of an experience that is beyond comprehension, and hold on to
it in the form of a self-in-relation-to-object-state" (Bollas 1987: 246). We
"know" such primordial experiences but cannot think them or speak of

them. We know them as a "felt sense" (the term is from Eugene Gendlin) of elation or dread, affirmation or negation. Such precursor experiences force themselves into awareness through fantasies, aesthetic experiences, the ways the subject relates to others, and transference. They may also be carried by the individual's religious longings and expressions. (I discuss in more detail the extensive relevance of Bollas' work for the psychology of religion in Jones 1991a: chap. 5.)

The human root of religious experience would thus be in the preverbal domain. The immediate appeal (or lack thereof) of certain religious images and symbols may be in part because they evoke (or fail to evoke) that "primordial" (Spero) or "unthought" (Bollas) realm of experience. In more traditional terms, the "imago Dei" of western theology or the "remembering soul" of Platonic and Neo-Platonic philosophy may well be found in the realm of preverbal experience. Part of the ineffable quality of religious experience may result from its tapping into the trace of a relationship that cannot be processed "through mental representation or language" (Bollas 1987: 3).

McDargh (1993) makes a distinction between two relational approaches to the psychoanalysis of religion: the "God relational" and the "faith relational" perspectives. Spero, says McDargh, illustrates the God relational approach, which "concerns itself with the complex correspondence between such object representations of 'God' and the individual's genuine, evolving relationship to what the client, and also the therapist, may be able to ontologically affirm as—and here language limps badly— the very God" (McDargh 1993: 183). The God relational perspective is explicitly theological in that it inquires after the specific contents of a person's belief. The faith relational perspective focuses "not upon the *what*, i.e., specific religious contents, but rather upon *how* the representational world functions, regardless of content" (1993: 183–184). Thus the "faith relational perspective attempts a more inclusive formulation of what constitutes 'religious material' in order to accommodate the widest range of human spiritual experience" (1993: 183). In academic terms, this perspective is less theological and more the product of a focus on religious studies or the study of comparative religions.

The strength of a God relational approach, like that of Spero, is that it meets the believer on his or her own terms and immediately accepts the fundamental premise of faith regarding the objectivity of the divine, however distorted by psychopathology may be any given individual's rendition of the divine. Such an approach makes sense for those therapists working in an explicitly denominational context, and for them, Spero's formulation of the divine object in terms of primordial consciousness and pre-established psychological structures provides a coherent psychological account of the place of the divine object in the human psyche. In addition, such a perspective, in contrast to more reductionistic approaches, takes seriously the ways religious experience can function as an independent, causal variable in people's lives (as illustrated by the case of Phil in chapter 3).

The faith relational perspective, however, by using a functional (rather than content-based) definition of religion, opens more material to psychoanalysis. The case of Maxine in chapter 3, for example, illustrates the application of relational techniques of interpretation to someone whose worldview contained virtually no traditionally religious content (the same can be said of the case of Martin in Jones 1991a). Such an approach seems clearly more useful for students and therapists working in a pluralistic or secular setting.

The God relational perspective, as illustrated by Spero, accepts too uncritically the dichotomy of subjectivity and objectivity (the same point is made in relation to Spero by Sorenson [1993]). Over and over Spero insists that religious belief requires assertion of a "veridical" God who is "objectively out there" (for example, "Religion views God as an *objective* [that is, real] aspect of reality" [1992: xv]). Certainly religious people from all traditions view the object of their devotion as real. But Spero holds the reality of religious (and psychoanalytic) knowledge too captive to a rigid dichotomy between objectivity and subjectivity.

Contemporary philosophy of science provides good reasons to question that rigid dichotomizing. The transitional sphere can possess ontological reality without sundering the world into "out there" and "in here" as though those were the only alternatives. Ironically, all objects of knowledge (whether in religion, psychoanalysis, or natural science) are *known* as objects only in a transitional, interactional space.

Conclusion
Being Human, Knowing God

I have suggested two possible alternatives to a reductionistic account of the relationship between psychoanalysis and religion: one involved compartmentalizing religion and science into separate disciplines; the other envisioned a hierarchical ordering of disciplines in terms of increasingly encompassing concerns. Each approach contains slightly different implications for the theological task and its relation to psychoanalysis. Framing the issue of science and religion in terms of compartmentalization continues the modern penchant for dichotomous reasoning. Envisioning the relationship between religion and science as increasingly more encompassing frames of reference introduces a potential continuity between them.

The first model begins from the idea that all disciplinary accounts are incomplete. Each is a self-contained, heuristic system within which claims are made and arguments advanced. Each has sharp boundaries that demarcate one field from another. Science neither threatens nor validates the claims of theology, as each field—drawing on its own domains of experiences, using its own methodologies, addressing its own unique questions—has its own theory autonomy. Such theological terms as *soul, spirit,* and *God* are constructs appropriate to a theological context, just as terms like *unconscious, repression,* or *denial* are appropriate to psychoanalysis and *curved space, neutrino,* or *vector* are appropriate to physics. Each set of terms is valuable to the extent that it helps us make sense of appropriate phenomena and answer appropriate questions.

Such an approach would emphasize the discontinuity between science—in this case psychoanalysis—and religion. Like the chemical and historical accounts of the painting, which neither disprove nor map onto each other, psychoanalytic and theological accounts of human nature or religious experience may each be considered valid in their own contexts (the only context in which an account can be valid). In this compartmentalized approach, conflict between psychoanalysis and religion is impossible, but dialogue is difficult, if not impossible, since there is no common language.

A second approach builds on the model of continuity between theology and psychology. Theological accounts are seen as continuous with psychodynamic and even neurobiological accounts of human nature and of religious experience. What distinguishes a theological account from a psychodynamic or neurobiological one is that it is more encompassing, just as an organic or systemic account of life processes is more encompassing than a strictly chemical one. To speak of the soul, the spirit, the divine is to speak of what encompasses but does not necessarily stand in opposition to the worlds of physics, biology, and psychology. Here such terms as *soul, spirit,* and *God* are not primarily seen as context-bound constructs but, rather, as the terms used to address the most encompassing and universal human concerns. The term *sacred* denotes what encompasses the ordinary world while not being reducible to the ordinary world.

Such a model of sacred reality stands in contrast to much modern Western theological thought. For a host of historical and cultural reasons, modern Western theology has emphasized discontinuity. Following modern science and modern philosophy, religion too has been captive to dichotomous reasoning: polarizing spirit and matter, soul and body, God and the world, by emphasizing the discontinuities between them (Jones 1984). In modernity, to speak of the soul, the spirit, or the divine is to point to what is outside of, over-against, the worlds of physics, biology, and psychology. Such a view of the sacred as completely separate from the finite world parallels the compartmentalized epistemology that sees religion as completely separate from science.

Behind these two approaches to religion and science—separate compartments or increasingly encompassing frameworks—lurk two different models of ultimate reality: that which stands apart from ordinary reality or that which encompasses or embraces ordinary reality. Having earlier cast some suspicion upon dichotomizing, I don't want to reintroduce it here at the end. We may well need both approaches to the relationship between science and religion and both models of the sacred. By itself, the way of compartmentalization preserves the integrity of both religion and psychoanalysis but at the price of any possible interdisciplinary discussion. Analogously it preserves the special nature of the divine but walls her unnaturally off from the rest of life.

In contrast, by itself the way of continuity can easily dissolve the crucial differences between religion and science into metaphysical mush and collapse the fierce mystery of the spirit into intellectually digestible and manipulable forms. A capacity to tolerate ambiguity enables one to hold in tension the way of compartmentalization and the way of continuity, for both are necessary for the dialogue between psychoanalysis and religion to take place. Jointly they provide enough distance between the disciplines and enough integrity to each discipline that neither can be reduced to the other, and jointly they also provide enough continuity and connection between the disciplines that discussion is possible.

This book thus concludes with one of the themes with which it began: the need to balance autonomy and connection. Kirkpatrick's three theological models of relationship—monism (representing the extreme of continuity), dualism (representing the extreme of separation), and pluralism (seeking a balance of the two)—could also be applied to the relations between religion and psychoanalysis. At one extreme all distinctions vanish and all disciplines collapse into one. This is the reductionist position, which claims that everything will be explained by physics or some other fundamental science. There may be a religious version of this position, which insists that all truth is found through a single sacred text or meditational practice. At the other extreme, disciplines are totally separate and distinct, with little interaction between them. In the middle is a pluralistic (Kirkpatrick's term) or relational model, in which disciplines interact and mutually influence each other while preserving their integrity.

A relational epistemology makes us aware of the common features of all forms of human understanding, psychoanalysis and theology included. All forms of understanding involve the "processing of symbols"

(Goodman) and the "metaphoric redescription" of experience (Lakoff and Johnson). All fields grow through the imaginative creation of categories and images (Arbib and Hesse). A relational epistemology underscores how all knowledge is transitional in a Winnicottian sense (Jones 1992a).

But the continuity between fields that arises from a relational epistemology is not a reduction of one field to another but a continuity in which disciplinary integrity is preserved. Like persons-in-relation, disciplines-in-relation interact with each other and mutually enrich each other. What emerges, than, from a relational epistemology is not some prefabricated synthesis of fields or Procrustian attempt to make all areas of knowledge resemble physics or mathematics or genetics. Rather, what emerges is an interactive dialogue in which the actual continuities and discontinuities, agreements and disagreements, cannot be predicted in advance. They become apparent only as the dialogue proceeds. With this book I invite psychoanalysts and theologians, therapists and spiritual practitioners, to take up that dialogue and discover various possible relationships between these two disciplines for themselves.

References

Allport, G. (1950). *The Individual and His Religion*. New York: Macmillan.

Arbib, M., and Hesse, M. (1986). *The Construction of Reality*. Cambridge: Cambridge University Press.

Aronson, H. (1985). "Guru Yoga—A Buddhist Meditative Visualization: Observations Based upon Psychoanalytic Object Relations Theory and Self Psychology." Paper presented to the annual meeting of the American Academy of Religion, Anaheim, Calif.

Beit-Hallahmi, B. (1992). "Between Religious Psychology and the Psychology of Religion." In *Object Relations Theory and Religion: Clinical Applications,* ed. M. Finn and J. Gartner. Westport, Conn.: Praeger.

Bergin, A. E. (1980). "Psychotherapy and Religious Values." *Journal of Consulting and Clinical Psychology* 48: 95–105.

Bernstein, R. (1988). *Beyond Objectivism and Relativism*. Philadelphia: University of Pennsylvania Press.

Bohm, D. (1957). *Causality and Chance in Modern Physics*. Philadelphia: University of Pennsylvania Press.

Bollas, C. (1989). *Forces of Destiny*. London: Free Association Press.

———. (1987). *The Shadow of the Object*. New York: Columbia University Press.

Brennan, T. (1992). *The Interpretation of the Flesh: Freud and Femininity*. New York: Routledge.

Brennan, T., ed. (1989). *Between Feminism and Psychoanalysis*. New York: Routledge.

Breuer, J., and Freud, S. (1893–1895). *Studies in Hysteria*. In *The Standard Edition of the Complete Psychological Works of S. Freud,* ed. James Strachey, 2: 1–305. London: Hogarth Press.

Browning, D. (1988). *Religious Thought and the Modern Psychologies*. Minneapolis: Fortress Press.

Buber, M. (1970). *I and Thou*. Trans. W. Kaufmann. New York: Scribners.

———. (1952). *The Eclipse of God*. New York: Harper and Row.

Chodorow, N. (1989). *Feminism and Psychoanalytic Theory*. New Haven: Yale University Press.

Christ, C. (1992). "Why Women Need the Goddess." In *Womanspirit Rising,* ed. C. Christ and J. Plaskow. San Francisco: HarperCollins.

Cobb, J. B., and Griffin, D. (1976). *Process Theology: An Introduction.* Philadelphia: Westminster Press.

Cuddihy, J. (1974). *The Ordeal of Civility.* New York: Basic Books.

Dawkins, R. (1987). *The Blind Watchmaker.* New York: Norton.

———. (1976). *The Selfish Gene.* Oxford: Oxford University Press.

Duncan, A. R. C. (1990). *On the Nature of Persons.* New York: Peter Lang.

Eller, C. (1993). *Living in the Lap of the Goddess.* New York: Crossroads.

Epstein, M. (1995). *Thoughts without a Thinker.* New York: Basic Books.

Erikson, E. (1968). *Identity: Youth and Crisis.* New York: Norton.

Fairbairn, W. R. D. (1954). "Observations on the Nature of Hysterical States." *British Journal of Medical Psychology* 27: 105–125.

———. (1952). *Psychoanalytic Studies of the Personality.* London: Routledge and Kegan Paul. Published in the United States in 1954 as *An Object Relations Theory of Personality.* New York: Basic Books.

Fingarette, H. (1963). *The Self in Transformation.* New York: Basic Books.

Finn, M. (1992). "Transitional Space and Tibetan Buddhism: The Object Relations of Meditation." In *Object Relations Theory and Religion: Clinical Applications,* ed. M. Finn and J. Gartner. Westport, Conn: Praeger.

Finn, M., and Gartner, J., eds. (1992). *Object Relations Theory and Religion: Clinical Applications.* Westport, Conn: Praeger.

Flax, J. (1993). *Disputed Subjects: Essays on Psychoanalysis, Politics and Philosophy.* New York: Routledge.

———. (1990). *Thinking Fragments: Psychoanalysis, Feminism, and Postmodernism in the Contemporary West.* Berkeley: University of California Press.

Freud, S. ([1940] 1948). *An Outline of Psychoanalysis.* New York: Norton.

———. ([1930] 1962). *Civilization and Its Discontents.* New York: Norton.

———. ([1927] 1964). *The Future of an Illusion.* Garden City, N.Y.: Doubleday Anchor.

———. ([1923] 1960). *The Ego and the Id.* New York: Norton.

———. ([1921] 1960). *Group Psychology and the Analysis of the Ego.* New York: Norton.

———. ([1920] 1959). *Beyond the Pleasure Principle.* New York: Bantam.

———. ([1913] 1950). *Totem and Taboo.* New York: Norton.

Gerhart, M., and Russell, A. (1984). *Metaphoric Process.* Fort Worth: Texas Christian University Press.

Gilligan, C. (1982). *In a Different Voice.* Cambridge: Harvard University Press.

Goldenberg, N. (1990). *Returning Words to Flesh.* Boston: Beacon Press.

———. (1979). *Changing of the Gods: Feminism and the End of Traditional Religions.* Boston: Beacon Press.

Goodman, N. (1984). *Of Mind and Other Matters.* Cambridge: Harvard University Press.

Greenberg, J., and Mitchell, S. (1983). *Object Relations in Psychoanalytic Theory.* Cambridge: Harvard University Press.

Grotstein, J., and Rinsley, D., eds. (1994). *Fairbairn and the Origins of Object Relations.* New York: Guilford Press.

Hare-Mustin, R., and Marecek, J., eds. (1990). *Making A Difference: Psychology and the Construction of Gender.* New Haven: Yale University Press.

Harlow, H., and Harlow, M. (1969). "Effects of Various Mother-Infant Relations of Rhesus Monkey Behaviors." In *Determinants of Infant Behavior,* vol. 4, ed. B. Foss. London: Metheuen.

Hartmann, H. (1960). *Psychoanalysis and Moral Values.* New York: International Universities Press.

———. (1958). *Ego Psychology and the Problem of Adaption.* New York: International Universities Press.

Hoffman, L. (1981). *Foundations of Family Therapy.* New York: Basic Books.

Homans, P. (1979). *Jung in Context: Modernity and the Making of a Psychology.* Chicago: University of Chicago Press.

———. (1970). *Theology after Freud: An Interpretive Inquiry.* New York: Irvington Press.

Hughes, J. (1994). "Fairbairn's Revision of Libido Theory: The Case of Harry Guntrip." In *Fairbairn and the Origins of Object Relations,* ed. J. Grotstein and D. Rinsley. New York: Guilford Press.

Jones, J. (in press a). "The Real Is the Relational: Relational Psychoanalysis as a Model of Human Understanding." In *Hermeneutical Approaches in the Psychology of Religion,* ed. J. A. van Belzen. Amersterdam: Rodopi.

———. (in press b). "Playing and Believing: The Uses of D. W. Winnicott in the Psychology of Religion." In *Religion, Society, and Psychoanalysis,* ed. J. Jacobs and D. Capps. Denver: Westview Press.

———. (1995). *In the Middle of This Road We Call Our Life.* San Francisco: HarperCollins.

———. (1992a). "Knowledge in Transition: Towards a Winnicottian Epistemology." *Psychoanalytic Review* 79, no. 2: 223–237.

———. (1992b). "Can Neuroscience Provide a Complete Account of Human Nature?" *Zygon: A Journal of Religion and Science* 27: 187–202.

———. (1991a). *Contemporary Psychoanalysis and Religion: Transference And Transcendence.* New Haven: Yale University Press.

———. (1991b). "The Relational Self: Contemporary Psychoanalysis Reconsiders Religion." *Journal of the American Academy of Religion* 59, no. 4: 501–517.

———. (1989). "Personality and Epistemology." *Zygon: A Journal of Religion and Science* 24: 23–38.

————. (1986). "Macrocosm to Microcosm: Towards a Systemic Theory of Personality." *Journal of Religion and Health* 25: 278–290.

————. (1984). *The Redemption of Matter: Towards the Rapprochement of Science and Religion*. Lanham, Md.: University Press of America.

————. (1982). "The Delicate Dialectic: Religion and Psychology in the Modern World." *Cross Currents* 32: 143–153.

————. (1981). *The Texture of Knowledge: An Essay on Religion and Science*. Lanham, Md.: University Press of America.

————. (1977). "The Lure of Fellowship." *Cross Currents* 26: 420–423.

————. (1972). "Reflections on the Problem of Religious Experience." *Journal of the American Academy of Religion* 40: 445–453.

Jones, J., and Goldenberg, N. (1992). *Transforming Psychoanalysis: Feminism and Religion*. Special issue of the *Journal of Pastoral Psychology* 40, no. 6.

Jonte-Pace, D. (1985). "Religion: A Rorschachian Projection Theory." *American Imago* 42: 199–234.

Kakar, S. (1991). *The Analyst and the Mystic*. Chicago: University of Chicago Press.

————. (1982). *Shamans, Mystics, and Doctors*. Chicago: University of Chicago Press.

Keller, E. F. (1992). *Secrets of Life, Secrets of Death: Essays on Language, Gender, and Science*. New York: Routledge.

————. (1985). *Reflections on Gender and Science*. New Haven: Yale University Press.

————. (1983). *A Feeling for the Organism: The Life and Work of Barbara McClintock*. New York: W. H. Freeman.

Keller, E. F., and Flax, J. (1988). "Missing Relations in Psychoanalysis: A Feminist Critique of Traditional and Contemporary Accounts of Analytic Theory and Practice." In *Hermeneutics and Psychological Theory*, ed. S. Messer, L. Sass, and R. Woolfolk. New Brunswick, N.J.: Rutgers University Press.

Kirkpatrick, F. G. (1994a). *Together Bound: God, History, and Religious Community*. New York: Oxford University Press.

————. (1994b). Personal correspondence dated September 14, 1994.

————. (1986). *Community: A Trinity of Models*. Washington, D.C.: Georgetown University Press.

————. (1970). *The Idea of God in the Thought of John Macmurray: Its Basis and Some Implications*. Ph.D. dissertation, Brown University.

Kohlberg, L. (1981). *The Philosophy of Moral Development*. New York: Harper and Row.

Kohut, H. (1984). *How Does Analysis Cure?* Chicago: University of Chicago Press.

————. (1977). *The Restoration of the Self*. New York: International Universities Press.

———. (1971). *The Analysis of the Self.* New York: International Universities Press.

Kuhn, T. (1972). *The Structure of Scientific Revolutions.* Chicago: University of Chicago Press.

Lakoff, G., and Johnson, M. (1980). *Metaphors We Live By.* Chicago: University of Chicago Press.

Layton, L. (1990). "A Deconstruction of Kohut's Concept of the Self." *Contemporary Psychoanalysis* 26: 420–429.

Leavy, S. (1988). *In the Image of God.* New Haven: Yale University Press.

———. (1986). "A Pascalian Meditation on Psychoanalysis and Religious Experience." *Cross Currents* 26: 147–155.

———. (1980). *Psychoanalytic Dialogue.* New Haven: Yale University Press.

Levinson, D. (1978). *Seasons of a Man's Life.* New York: Ballantine.

Lichtenberg, J. (1991). "What Is A Selfobject?" *Psychoanalytic Dialogues* 1: 455–479.

———. (1983). *Psychoanalysis and Infant Research.* Hillsdale, N.J.: Analytic Press.

Loewald, H. (1988). *Sublimation.* New Haven: Yale University Press.

———. (1980). *Papers on Psychoanalysis.* New Haven: Yale University Press.

———. (1978). *Psychoanalysis and the History of the Individual.* New Haven: Yale University Press.

Lutzky, H. (1991). "The Sacred and the Maternal Object: An Application of Fairbairn's Theory to Religion." In *Psychoanalytic Reflections on Current Issues,* ed. H. Seigel. New York: New York University Press.

Macmurray, J. (1961). *Persons in Relation.* London: Faber and Faber.

———. (1957). *The Self as Agent.* London: Faber and Faber.

———. (1938). *The Clue to History.* London: SCM Press.

Malony, N., and Spilka, B. (1991). *Religion in Psychodynamic Perspective: The Contributions of Paul W. Pruyser.* New York: Oxford University Press.

McDargh, J. (1993). "Concluding Clinical Postscript: On Developing a Psychotheological Perspective." In *Exploring Sacred Landscapes: Religious and Spiritual Experiences in Psychotherapy,* ed. M. L. Randour. New York: Columbia University Press.

———. (1988). "Beyond God as Transitional Object." Paper presented to a meeting of the College Theology Society, Los Angeles, California.

———. (1983). *Psychoanalytic Object Relations Theory and the Study of Religion.* Lanham, Md.: University Press of America.

McFague, S. (1988). *Models of God.* Philadelphia: Fortress Press.

Meissner, W. W. (1990). "The Role of Transitional Conceptualizations in Religious Thought." In *Psychoanalysis and Religion,* ed. J. Smith and S. Handelman. Baltimore: Johns Hopkins University Press.

————. (1984). *Psychoanalysis and Religious Experience.* New Haven: Yale University Press.

Merchant, C. (1980). *The Death of Nature.* San Francisco: Harper and Row.

Messer, S., Sass, L., and Woolfolk, R. (1988). *Hermeneutics and Psychological Theory.* New Brunswick, N.J.: Rutgers University Press.

Miller, J. B. (1976). *Toward a New Psychology of Women.* Boston: Beacon Press.

Minuchin, S. (1974). *Families and Family Therapy.* Cambridge: Harvard University Press.

Mitchell, S. (1993). *Hope and Dread in Psychoanalysis.* New York: Basic Books.

————. (1991). "Contemporary Perspectives on Self: Towards an Integration—Paper and Discussion." *Psychoanalytic Dialogues* 1: 121–180.

————. (1990). "True Selves, False Selves, and the Ambiguity of Authenticity." Paper presented to the Westchester Institute for Psychoanalysis, White Plains, N.Y., December.

————. (1988). *Relational Concepts in Psychoanalysis.* Cambridge: Harvard University Press.

Moi, T. (1989). "Patriarchal Thought and the Drive for Knowledge." In *Between Feminism and Psychoanalysis,* ed. T. Brennan. New York: Routledge.

Nietzsche, F. (1954). "The Genealogy of Morals" (1887). In *The Philosophy of Nietzsche.* New York: Random House.

Ornstein, P. (1991). "Why Self Psychology Is Not an Object Relations Theory." In *The Evolution of Self Psychology: Progress in Self Psychology,* ed. A. Goldberg, 7: 17–30. Hillsdale, N.J.: Analytic Press.

Otto, R. (1958). *The Idea of the Holy.* Trans. J. W. Harvey. New York: Oxford University Press.

Phillips, A. (1988). *Winnicott.* Cambridge: Harvard University Press.

Polanyi, M. (1974). *Personal Knowledge.* New York: Harper and Row.

Pruyser, P. (1974). *Between Belief and Unbelief.* New York: Harper and Row.

————. (1968). *A Dynamic Psychology of Religion.* New York: Harper and Row.

Rainey, R. (1975). *Freud as a Student of Religion.* AAR Dissertation Series 7. Missoula, Mont.: Scholars Press.

Randour, M. L., ed. (1993). *Exploring Sacred Landscapes: Religious and Spiritual Experiences in Psychotherapy.* New York: Columbia University Press.

Rieff, P. (1959). *Freud: The Mind of the Moralist.* New York: Viking Press.

Rizzuto, A.-M. (1979). *The Birth of the Living God.* Chicago: University of Chicago Press.

Robert, M. (1976). *From Oedipus to Moses: Freud's Jewish Identity.* Trans. R. Manheim. Garden City, N.Y.: Doubleday Anchor.

Saur, M., and Saur, W. (1993). "Transitional Phenomena as Evidenced in Prayer." *Journal of Religion and Health* 32: 1.

————. (n.d.). *Manual for the STARR.* N.p.

Schafer, R. (1976). *A New Language for Psychoanalysis*. New Haven: Yale University Press.

Smith, J., and Handelman, S. (1990). *Psychoanalysis and Religion*. Baltimore: Johns Hopkins University Press.

Smith, R. S. (1985). "The Becoming of the Person in Martin Buber's Religious Philosophical Anthropology and Heinz Kohut's Psychology of the Self." Ph.D. dissertation, University of Chicago.

Socarides, D., and Stolorow, R. (1984–85). "Affects and Selfobjects." *Annual of Psychoanalysis* 12–13: 105–119. New York: International Universities Press.

Sorenson, A. (1990). "Psychoanalytic Perspectives on Religion: The Illusion Has a Future," *Journal of Psychology and Theology* 18: 209–217.

Sorenson, R. (1994). "Ongoing Change in Psychoanalytic Theory: Implications for Analysis of Religious Experience" and "Reply to Spezzano." *Psychoanalytic Dialogues* 4: 631–660, 667–672.

———. (1993). "What If God Is Not a Klienian Mother? A Review of M. H. Spero, *Religious Objects as Psychological Structures*," *Journal of Psychology and Theology* 21: 249–254.

Spence, D. (1987). *The Freudian Metaphor: Toward Paradigm Change in Psychoanalysis*. New York: Norton.

———. (1982). *Narrative and Historical Truth*. New York: Norton.

Spero, M. H. (1992). *Religious Objects as Psychological Structures: A Critical Integration of Object Relations Theory, Psychotherapy, and Judaism*. Chicago: University of Chicago Press.

———. (1990). "Parallel Dimensions of Experience in Psychoanalytic Psychotherapy of the Religious Patient." *Psychotherapy* 27: 53–71.

Spilka, B., Addison, J., and Rosensohn, M. (1975). "Parents, Self and God: A Test of Competing Theories of Individual-Religion Relationships." *Review of Religious Research* 16: 154–165.

Spilka, B., Armatas, P., and Nussbaum, J. (1964). "The Concept of God: A Factor-Analytic Approach." *Review of Religious Research* 6: 20–35.

Stern, D. N. (1985). *The Interpersonal World of the Infant*. New York: Basic Books.

Stolorow, R. (1992). "Closing the Gap between Theory and Practice with Better Psychoanalytic Theory." *Psychotherapy* 29: 159–166.

Stolorow, R., and Atwood, G. (1991). "The Mind and the Body." *Psychoanalytic Dialogues* 1: 181–196.

———. (1984). "Psychoanalytic Phenomenology: Toward a Science of Human Experience." *Psychoanalytic Inquiry* 4: 87–105.

———. (1979). *Faces in a Cloud: Subjectivity in Personality Theory*. New York: Jason Aronson.

Stolorow, R., Brandchaft, B., and Atwood, G. (1987). *Psychoanalytic Treatment: An Intersubjective Approach*. New York: Analytic Press.

———. (1985). Untitled. Paper presented to the Eighth Annual Conference on Self Psychology, New York.

———. (1983). "Intersubjectivity in Psychoanalytic Treatment." *Bulletin of the Menninger Clinic* 47: 117–128.

Stolorow, R., and Lachmann, F. (1985). "Transference: The Future of an Illusion." In *Annual of Psychoanalysis,* vols. 12–13. New York: International Universities Press.

———. (1980). *Psychoanalysis of Developmental Arrests.* New York: International Universities Press.

Summers, F. (1994). *Object Relations Theories and Psychopathology.* Hillsdale, N.J.: Analytic Press.

Sutherland, J. (1989). *Fairbairn's Journey into the Interior.* London: Free Association Press.

Tillich, P. (1957). *The Dynamics of Faith.* New York: Harper and Row.

———. (1952). *The Courage to Be.* New Haven: Yale University Press.

———. (1951). *Systematic Theology,* vol. 1. Chicago: University of Chicago Press.

Toulmin, S. (1960). *The Philosophy of Science.* New York: Harper and Row.

Van Herik, J. (1982). *Freud on Femininity and Faith.* Berkeley: University of California Press.

Vergote, A., and Aubert, C. (1972). "Parental Images and Representations of God." *Social Compass* 19: 431–444.

Vergote, A., Tamyo, A., Pasquali, L., Bonami, M., Pattyn, A., and Custers, A. (1969). "The Concept of God and Parental Images." *Journal of the Scientific Study of Religion* 8:79–87.

Wallwork, E. (1991). *Psychoanalysis and Ethics.* New Haven: Yale University Press.

Weber, M. (1991). *The Protestant Ethic and the Spirit of Capitalism* (1904). New York: HarperCollins.

Whitehead, A. N. (1929). *Process and Reality.* New York: Macmillan.

Winnicott, D. W. (1989). *Psychoanalytic Explorations.* Cambridge: Harvard University Press.

———. (1988). *Human Nature.* New York: Schocken Books.

———. (1975). *Through Paediatrics to Psychoanalysis.* New York: Basic Books.

———. (1971). *Playing and Reality.* New York: Routledge.

———. (1965). *The Maturational Process and the Facilitating Environment.* London: Hogarth.

Wright, R. (1994). *The Moral Animal: The New Science of Evolutionary Psychology.* New York: Pantheon Books.

Index

Arbib, M., 111–112, 144

Beit-Hallahmi, B., 44
Bernstein, R., 107–109
Bollas, C., 128–130, 148
Buber, M.: theory of relationships, 69–74, 83, 92, 144; compared with Kohut, 70–72
Buddhism, 43, 45, 66–68, 92

Chodorow, N., 8, 10, 87, 125–126
Civilization and Its Discontents (Freud), 18–21, 131–132

Ego and the Id, The (Freud), 3–11

Fairbairn, W. R. D.: relational theory, 24–25, 28–35, 65–66, 99; and Macmurray, 27–28, 32; and Kohut, 38–39
Feminist psychoanalytic theory, 10, 86, 124–127
Feminist theology, 14–16, 17–18, 87–88
Freud, S.: views on human nature, 3–23; and Rolland, 6, 15–16, 67–68, 84; sublimation, 20–21; drive theory, 21, 28–32; Fairbairn's critique of, 28–35; and Kohut, 36–38; on religion, 67–68, 98–100, 114; on narcissism, 97–98, 100; mentioned, 102, 106, 107, 124, 127
Future of an Illusion, The (Freud), 98–100

Gender: Freud's theories of, 4–10, 14–18; in feminist psychoanalytic theory, 10–11; and religion, 14–18, 86, 87–88; and human knowledge, 124–127

God: Freud's theory about, 13–18; Buber's approach to, 69–74; idea of a personal God, 72–74, 74–77, 87–88, 92, 94; Macmurray's philosophy of, 74–77; Kirkpatrick's models of, 77–80, 82; in feminist theology, 87–88; in process theology, 89–91
God representation, internal, 41–46, 51–53, 145–147
Goddess religion, 87–88
Goodman, N., 108–109

Hesse, M., 111–112, 144
Hinduism, 43, 45, 67–68, 92

Illusion: Freud on, 98–100; Winnicott's theory of, 106–107; Prusyer on, 138–140; discussed by Meissner and Rizzuto, 140–143
Intersubjective psychoanalytic theory, 38–40, 46, 65–68

Johnson, M., 109–111, 144

Kirkpatrick, F. G.: models of God, 77–82, 86–88; on Whitehead, 90–91; on the idea of a personal God, 92–94; mentioned, 27, 83, 86, 153
Kohut, H.: theory of self psychology, 35–40; on religion, 44; compared with Buber, 70–72; mentioned, 41, 44, 67, 83, 85, 92

Lakoff, G., 109–111, 144
Layton, L., 38, 72, 126

Lichtenberg, J., 38–39, 46, 85
Loewald, H.: on subjectivity and objectivity, 104–107; critique of Winnicott, 105–106; theory of religious symbols, 131–133, 135–136

Macmurray, J.: relational philosophy, 25–28; relation to Fairbairn, 27–28, 32, 35; approach to God, 39, 74–77, 92–94; and Buber, 69; and Kirkpatrick, 79, 82; mentioned, 83, 99, 123, 144
McDargh, J., 27, 44, 144–145, 149–150
McFague, S., 87–88, 92–94
Meissner, W. W.: quoted, 106; theory of religious symbols, 136–137, 138; use of idea of transitional objects, 140–142
Mitchell, S., 5, 22, 38, 66

Narcissism, 97–98, 100
Nietzsche, F., 20–21

Objectivity. See Subject-object dualism
Oedipus complex, 4–18, 21–22, 31–32

Patriarchal culture and religion, 7–9, 13–18, 126
Process theology, 89–91
Pruyser, P., 138–140

Reductionism: critiques of, 25–27, 115–123; psychodynamics of, 123–130; alternatives to, 131–138, 145–150
Relational psychoanalytic theory: and Macmurray's philosophy, 25–27; Fairbairn's, 28–35; Kohut's, 35–40; and religious experience, 41–46, 65–69; implications for theology, 82–87; Winnicott's, 101–103; as an epistemology, 140–144, 153–154
Rizzuto, A.-M.: theory of God representation, 41–44, 146; use of idea of transi-

tional objects, 138–139, 140, 142–143; mentioned, 52
Rolland, R., 6, 15–16, 67–68, 84

Self psychology. See Kohut, H.
Selfobjects, theory of, 35–39, 41–42, 45, 70
Smith, R. S., 71–72
Spero, M. H., 44, 145–150
Stolorow, R., 38–39, 46, 65–66
Subjectivity, 38–40, 65–68. See also Subject-object dualism
Subject-object dualism: in Winnicott, 102–103, 126–127, 133–134; in Loewald, 105–106; in contemporary philosophy, 107–113; in Pruyser, 138–140; in relational theory, 140–144, 150
Superego, 3–11, 19–22

Tillich, P., 91–93, 107
Totem and Taboo (Freud), 11–18
Transitional phenomena: in Winnicott, 101–103, 106–107, 110–113, 133–136; epistemological implications of, 107–113, 133–136, 138–145, 150; loss of capacity for, 129–130; religious symbols as, 133–138; used by Meissner and Rizzuto, 136–138; used by Pruyser, 138–140; meaning of, 140–144

Van Herik, J., xi, 6, 9

Wallwork, E., 17, 21
Weber, M., 19–20
Whitehead, A. N., 89–91
Winnicott, D. W.: theory of transitional phenomena, 100–103, 129, 133–136; compared with Loewald, 105–107; epistemological implications of work of, 110–113, 140–144; theory of symbols, 133–136; used by Meissner and Rizzuto, 136–138, 140–144; used by Pruyser, 138–140; mentioned, 28, 32, 33, 65, 83, 99